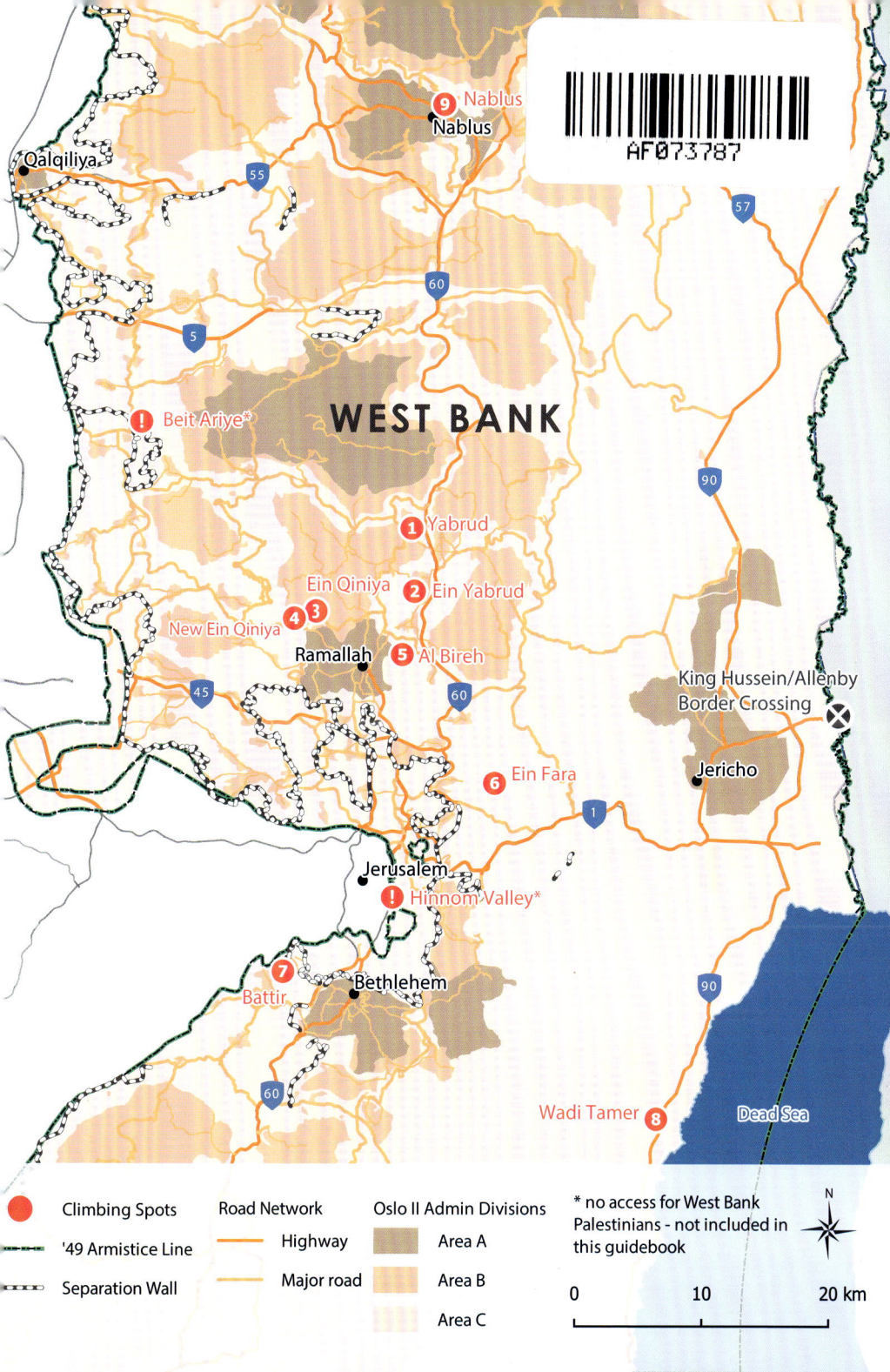

IMPRINT

Authors: Bruns, Korff & Moser
Design: Esther Strunck
Maps: Benjamin Korff

All rights reserved.
Copyright © 2019

1st Edition October 2019
ISBN 978-1-947474-16-1

DISCLAIMER: Rock climbing is an inherently dangerous activity. Conditions are subject to change and may not be the same on the ground as described in this book. Every effort has been made by the authors to be accurate, but there may be inaccuracies in the book. Any use of the information provided in this book is at the users' own risk. The political situation in Palestine can change rapidly. Readers should check the local conditions before visiting any of the climbing areas.

Cover photo: Urwah Askar on "Pickpocket," 7b in Yabrud | Photo by Markus Maier

CLIMBING PALESTINE
A guide to rock climbing in the West Bank

Tim Bruns | Ben Korff | Albert Moser

TABLE OF CONTENTS

Foreword 04
The History of Rock Climbing in Palestine 05
On Climbing and Politics in Palestine 06
A Brief History of the Conflict 08
The Current Situation 11
Practical Tips 12
Wadi Climbing Gym 20
Nature and Geology 21

CLIMBING AREAS

01	Yabrud	26
02	Ein Yabrud	48
03	Ein Qiniya	56
04	New Ein Qiniya (Under the Ruins)	72
05	Al Bireh (Maktabna)	80
06	Ein Fara	86
07	Battir	116
08	Wadi Tamer	126
	Wadi Tamer Bouldering	132
09	Nablus	138

Route Index 147
Map Legend 155

Nina Caprez on "Tannourine Dream," 7b (page 35)
Photo by Sam Challiet

FOREWORD

WHY A PALESTINE CLIMBING GUIDEBOOK?

When you strip away everything non-essential about climbing—that is equipment, ego, grades—climbing is in its essence about movement. Just like swimming or running, rock climbing moves us through unique environments and takes us to places where we could otherwise not go. By learning how to climb rocks, we expand our freedom of movement.

Freedom of movement is at the core of our motivation to author this guidebook. In many places around the world, freedom of movement is taken for granted. Most people are free to move around their own country and to explore its natural environments. This is not the case in Palestine. Decades of conflict and the Israeli occupation of the West Bank have led to a system of structural domination that inhibits the freedom of movement for most Palestinians. This makes climbing access a sensitive and complicated issue, often keeping Palestinian climbers from visiting spots that are located close to their homes, deep within Palestinian territory.

Despite this troubling context, visitors will find incredible rock climbing in idyllic landscapes and a growing community of enthusiastic and welcoming local climbers. By showcasing what the West Bank has to offer, we hope to encourage international climbers to visit and experience the richness of this place through the medium of rock climbing.

We felt that it was necessary to publish a guidebook that covers areas accessible to Palestinian climbers. The vast majority of crags in this book are brand new climbing locations in the West Bank that were recently developed by the authors and local climbers. Some climbing areas that we feature can also be found in the Israel Climbing Guidebook (Nachmias and Shadmi 2015) although Palestinian climbers are not able to reach the majority of crags in that guidebook. For those areas, our guidebook provides additional background information that gives visiting international climbers a better feel for what it means to climb in Palestine.

By publishing this guidebook, we hope to put Palestine and its amazing rock on the international climbing map, encourage foreigners to visit and climb in Palestine, and advocate for increased freedom of movement for Palestinians.

Let this be clear from the beginning: the contributors to this book sympathize with the Palestinian people and their daily struggles under occupation. Any accounts given in this book are based on our subjective impressions and experiences, and thus we do not claim objectivity. Nevertheless, we have made every effort to ensure that this book makes factual claims backed by widely-accepted evidence, such as official statistics and reports.

The authors, August 2019.

INTRODUCTION

THE HISTORY OF ROCK CLIMBING IN PALESTINE

Nomadic Bedouin have been scrambling the rocky landscape of Palestine for centuries. The first modern rock climbing started in the mid-seventies in the Hinnom Valley, just outside the Old City of Jerusalem, when two visiting climbers from the US started putting up routes on a small cliff that can still be climbed today. (The rock is more polished than your grandma's silver.) A few years later, during the late seventies, the Ein Fara area of Wadi Qelt (see chapter 6), a steep valley on the way to Jericho from Jerusalem, was discovered for climbing. The first bolts were put into the wall in 1982 by Andrea Anati (Jigsaw Puzzle, 6b). It was not until a couple of years ago that Palestinians Marwan Tarazi and Hani Thaher began setting up top ropes on the cliffs near Ein Qiniya village and inviting friends and family to climb with them.

In June of 2014, Tim Bruns (author) and Will Harris, two American climbers from Colorado, moved to Ramallah with the idea to establish the first indoor climbing gym in Palestine: Wadi Climbing. Their vision was to leverage rock climbing as a tool for social empowerment in a place with few recreational opportunities. While looking for investors and a location for the gym, Tim and Will received a modest grant to start developing some outdoor sport climbing routes in area "A" of the West Bank. After hearing some rumors about Marwan Tarazi, they took a hike with Wahid Masri near Ein Qiniya village and spotted the cliffs that would become one of the staple climbing areas for climbers from Ramallah. The first route bolted was "Yom Asel" 6a+ (translation: Day of Honey).

After establishing a number of moderate climbs in Ein Qiniya, Wadi Climbing began to hold introductory climbing trips for beginners to build enthusiasm for the sport before opening the gym. Within months, more climbing potential was discovered at the cliffs in Yabrud and Ein Yabrud. Climbing development started shortly thereafter. In March 2016, with the help of climbing gym owners from Colorado and the growing local climbing community, Wadi Climbing, a bouldering gym, was opened to the public. To this day, Wadi Climbing has led hundreds of outdoor climbing trips, and thousands of people have learned to climb on trips and in the gym. With the contributions and dedication of both foreign and local climbers, over 170 new sport climbing routes have been bolted at sites around the West Bank, making it a wonderful climbing destination for climbers of all abilities! Perhaps the most inspiring development has been the consistent growth of the local Palestinian climbing community. The visiting climber will find a warm, enthusiastic, and diverse group of locals who climb at various crags around the West Bank throughout the year. We encourage you to seek out the locals, swap belays, learn a little Arabic, and maybe even try some of the Qalayat Bandoora (fried tomatoes) that often gets cooked over an open fire at the crags.

INTRODUCTION

ON CLIMBING AND POLITICS IN PALESTINE

As with anything in Palestine, climbing is a political act. Access to climbing areas often depends on your nationality and ethnicity. Where and with whom we climb can be interpreted as a political statement whether we mean it to be or not.

While international visitors can go almost everywhere in the "Holy Land," Israelis and Palestinians will rarely meet at a climbing crag that is safely accessible to both. Thus, the authors of this guidebook believe that, unfortunately, it is impossible to separate climbing from politics and feel that it is important to provide some historical context as well as a short description of the current political situation in Palestine.

Due to the complexity of the situation, this description will necessarily remain superficial, sometimes simplistic, and certainly informed by personal experience. We encourage anyone to listen to both sides, read up on the vast literature available, and make up their own mind.

TERMINOLOGY: PALESTINE OR WEST BANK?

The word Palestine is used differently at times to refer to the West Bank and the Gaza Strip and/or the entire historical land of Palestine (pre-1948). There is no rock climbing in the Gaza Strip and access for outsiders is near impossible. As such, in this guidebook we use the word Palestine usually to refer to the West Bank. Many readers may know that the use of the word "Palestine" in itself can be viewed as a political statement, though the term is widely accepted by the majority of the international community.

Hikers on the Abraham Path hiking trail near Hebron
Photo by Frits Meyst

Tim Bruns bolting in Yabrud
Photo by Dario Franchetti

INTRODUCTION

A BRIEF HISTORY OF THE CONFLICT

All climbing spots in this guidebook (as well as those in the *Israel Cimbing Guidebook*) are located in disputed territory claimed by both Israelis and Palestinians and are shaped by a century of conflict.

The Israeli-Palestinian conflict is intimately connected to the European colonization of the Middle East. The Sykes-Picot agreement of 1916 effectively divided the Ottoman Empire between France and Great Britain, settling geopolitical and colonial spheres of influence at the end of World War I in 1918. The land between the Jordan River and the Mediterranean Sea became British territory known as Mandate Palestine. In 1917, with the Balfour Declaration, the British Government declared its support for the Zionist movement, which sought to build a "national home for the Jewish people" in Mandate Palestine. In response to rising anti-Semitism in Europe, support for Zionism increased among the Jewish population in Europe in the late 19th century. The first European Jewish settlers moved to Ottoman-ruled Palestine during the *First Aliyah* immigration in the 1890s. In the early 20th century, Jewish immigration continued and conflicts between the native Arab population and Zionist settlers became more frequent. While the British government did try to regulate immigration, the rise of fascism in Europe and the atrocities committed against Jews by Nazi Germany and its allies further strengthened Zionist sentiment and led to an influx of Jewish settlers and refugees to the region.

The end of World War II saw mass immigration of European Jews to Mandate Palestine, which the British were unable to control. In the wake of this immigration, David Ben Gurion declared Israeli Independence in 1947, which directly led to the first Arab-Israeli War and the forcible transfer of large parts of the Arab population in Mandate Palestine. Roughly 750,000 Palestinians left their homes and were not allowed to return when the fighting was over. This constituted the creation of the modern State of Israel and is referred to as the "Nakba" (catastrophe) by Palestinians. Palestinian refugees ended up all over the world, and many still live in refugee camps in the Palestinian Territories (the West Bank and Gaza Strip) and surrounding Arab countries (Jordan, Lebanon, Syria, etc).

The State of Israel became further established, further cementing the situation for Palestinians refugees, now living in United Nations-managed refugee camps. Subsequent decades and Israeli military victories over its Arab neighbor (Six-Day War 1967, Yom Kippur War 1973, Lebanon War 1982) further strengthened Israel's position in the region and led to further territory falling under Israeli control, including East Jerusalem, the West Bank, the Golan Heights, and the Sinai Peninsula (later returned to Egypt). Increasing repression against Palestinians—including house demolitions, destruction of agricultural land, arbitrary arrests, and "administrative detentions" without trial—led to the outbreak of the *First Intifada* (Arabic for "uprising") in 1987, which attracted unprecedented international attention to the Palestinian struggle and paved the road to the Oslo Accords of 1993 and 1995. As an outcome of the Oslo Accords, the Palestinian Authority (PA) was founded as an interim governmental body for the Palestinian people. Accordingly, the West Bank was divided into Areas A and B, to be under full or partial Palestinian control, as well as Area C, where Israel remained the sole authority in both civil and military matters. This division pended further negotiations that would lead to an independent Palestinian state with sovereignty over its land. Negotiations proceeded slowly and took a severe hit after the assassination of the Israeli Prime Minister Yitzhak Rabin in 1995.

The failure of the Camp David Summit in 2000 simultaneously marked the failure of the Oslo peace process and the beginning of the Second Intifada, a time of intensified tension and violence between the Israeli military and Palestinians, which formally ended in 2005.

During the *Second Intifada*, the Israeli government started construction of the separation wall, which still crisscrosses through and around the West Bank. Intended to secure Israel from aggression from within the West Bank, the wall remains incomplete,

currently unbolted' ;-)
A climber on the perfect hand jams of the Separation Wall in Bethlehem
Photo by Julie Ellison

INTRODUCTION

cutting through large sections of the West Bank, effectively annexing large swaths of Palestinian land. The last decade has brought more of the same: systematic oppression of Palestinians, three wars in Gaza, numerous smaller uprisings across the West Bank, and increasing confiscation of Palestinian land by Israeli settlements, with no solution on the horizon.

INTRODUCTION

THE CURRENT SITUATION

United Nations map of Jerusalem
Photo by Sam Challeat

Life for most Palestinians in the West Bank has grown slowly and steadily less free since 1948. The 1967 war marked the beginning of Israel's occupation of the West Bank and Gaza Strip. Since then, life in the occupied Palestinian territory has been disrupted by Israeli military measures, including restrictions in freedom of movement, forcible transfer of Palestinians, destruction of property, and the devastating increase in state-sponsored illegal settlements. The word "illegal" is used because the Fourth Geneva Convention prohibits an occupying power from colonizing the land that it occupies.[1] As of December 2017, over 611,000[2] Israeli citizens resided in the West Bank and East Jerusalem, made possible through a government program of considerable subsidies, free services, and tax breaks for living in a settlement.[3] The result is a situation in which the State of Israel, for all intents and purposes, maintains full control of most of the West Bank but does not offer equal rights to the Palestinians under its control.[4] The PA, a relic of the Oslo Accords of 1993 (I) and 1995 (II), holds a small degree of control over parts of the West Bank and Gaza but is often criticized for its corruption and collaboration with the Israeli security apparatus. Being dependent on foreign aid and tax transfers from the Israeli government, the PA has little leverage and political will to forward an agenda that could bring about positive change for the Palestinian people. A complicated system of permits, identification papers, barriers, checkpoints, policing, and surveillance leaves no room for Palestinian self-determination or national sovereignty.

For better or worse, life under the PA in cities like Ramallah is liveable and, for foreign visitors, quite safe. Tourists and visitors, who have the privilege of a foreign passport, can freely, and generally safely, navigate in Palestine and Israel. It is within this context that rock climbing plays a complex and sometimes liberating role.

---

[1] Article 49 of the Fourth Geneva Convention states
"The occupying power shall not deport or transfer parts of its own population into the territories it occupies."
[2] https://www.ochaopt.org/sites/default/files/israeli_settlement_activities.pdf
[3] OHCHR fact finding report to UN Resolution 19/17:
https://www.ohchr.org/Documents/HRBodies/HRCouncil/RegularSession/Session19/FFM/FFMSettlements.pdf
[4] Under the Fourth Geneva Convention, any Occupying Power must rule for the benefit of the protected population – in this instance, the Palestinians.

PRACTICAL TIPS

TRAVELING TO AND FROM PALESTINE
Palestine is occupied by the state of Israel, so any visitor to Palestine will need to enter through an Israeli border. Many nationalities, including European and US passport holders, are issued an Israeli tourist visa on arrival valid for three months. All climbing spots in this guidebook are located in the West Bank, so we will not discuss the complicated process of gaining access to the Gaza Strip. Most travelers to the West Bank fly into Ben Gurion airport near Tel Aviv. It is also possible to enter overland via Jordan or Egypt, though this adds the hassle and cost of land transportation.

THE BORDER
Israeli security at airports and land borders is very tight and wary of individual travelers (not in a tour group), especially those who state an intention to visit Palestine. We recommend exercising a certain degree of discretion in what you disclose about your travel plans at the border. Do not lie, but provide only the information that is requested. It's a good idea to emphasize some of the more typical tourist destinations in the area without mentioning Palestine or the West Bank. Travelers have been questioned intensely and even barred entry if they are suspected of engaging in political activism.

Important tip: Do no lose the blue paper visa that you are issued at the border; you will need it while crossing in and out of the West Bank!

RAMALLAH
This guidebook focuses mostly on the surroundings of Ramallah, the commercial and de facto political capital of the West Bank, because the vast majority of the developed climbing in the West Bank is around the city. Therefore, most of our suggestions for travel, eating, and lodging are in Ramallah.

Originally a small Christian village, Ramallah has grown exponentially in the past decades. After the "Nakba" of 1948, many Palestinian refugees fleeing conflict in other areas of the country ended up in Ramallah. The city experienced another large period of growth after the establishment of the PA in 1994 and the subsequent increase in job opportunities. Today, the greater city's population is roughly 200,000 people (including the surrounding municipalities and villages).

Ramallah is a relatively cosmopolitan city with a large number of expats mostly working as journalists, development workers, and diplomats. There are plenty of cultural and culinary places to discover to complement your rock climbing activities!

GETTING TO RAMALLAH IN THE WEST BANK

From Ben Gurion Airport, take a "sherut" (shared mini bus) to Jerusalem and ask the driver to drop you off at the Jerusalem Hotel near the Damascus Gate of the Old City. The ride should cost around 75 NIS. The bus station for Ramallah is situated directly across the street from the Jerusalem Hotel. You can also take Egged bus 485 from Ben Gurion Airport to the West Jerusalem bus station, which runs hourly day and night every day except Saturday (~16NIS). Alternatively, take the newly-constructed high speed train from Ben Gurion to the Yitzhak Navon station in West Jerusalem (your first trip is free). Ride the light rail from the stop across the street from Yitzhak Navon station eastwards to the Damascus Gate station (6 stops, ~8 NIS). Walk from the Damascus Gate light rail station to the bus station across from the Jerusalem Hotel. From there take the bus 218/219 to Ramallah (~8 NIS). When the bus departs, it will head north through East Jerusalem and eventually cross through the Qalandia military checkpoint and continue on to central Ramallah. The bus ride takes 30 minutes to an hour depending on checkpoint traffic. Stay on the bus all the way until the last stop at the central bus station in downtown Ramallah.

Important note: Buses, pedestrians, and cars entering the West Bank are normally not checked at checkpoints. Remember that when leaving the West Bank through the Qalandia or other checkpoints you will be stopped and asked to present your passport and visa to Israeli border control.

Qalandia Checkpoint
Photo by Esther Strunck

PRACTICAL TIPS

FROM JORDAN
ALLENBY / KING HUSSEIN BRIDGE
The most direct way to access the West Bank from Jordan is by crossing the Allenby/King Hussein Bridge border. Opening hours, rules, and regulations for travel over the bridge are subject to change and are sometimes unclear. For the latest information, check online (www.iaa.gov.il/en-US/borders/alenbi/Pages/default.aspx) and read accounts by people on TripAdvisor.

CURRENCY
The currency used in the West Bank is the New Israeli Shekel (NIS). Some places also accept Jordanian Dinar (JOD).

EUR	NIS	JOD
1	3.9	0.79

USD	NIS	JOD
1	3.50	0.71

(current as of August 2019)

HEALTH & EMERGENCY
In case of an emergency, dial 101. This number will route to Israeli or Palestinian emergency services depending on your location. In case of an emergency where it takes too long for an ambulance to arrive, we recommend driving yourself or taking a taxi or service—the drivers will know about the closest hospital or doctor.

Pharmacies are generally well stocked with most common medicines. It's a good idea to bring a copy of your prescription along if you regularly take a prescription medicine.

PHARMACIES IN RAMALLAH
Al-Barghouthi Pharmacy
Latin Convent Building. Al-Ahliyyah College St, opposite to Solo Gym

Old Ramallah Pharmacy
Near the Greek Orthodox Church, Ramallah Tahta, diagonally behind the gas station

Pharma One Pharmacy
Rebhi Al-Hajjah Building, Irsal Street, near Muqata'a

VACCINATIONS
No vaccinations are officially required for travel, though standard vaccinations are recommended. You can find more important information on the website of the Center for Travel Medicine (www.crm.de/).

HOSPITALS IN RAMALLAH
Istishari Arab Hospital
Al-Rayhan Suburb (near Ein Qiniya)
http://www.iah.ps/welcome/index/en
info@iah.ps | Tel +970 2 2943 200

Arabcare Hospital
Al Nahda St., Ramallah
arabcare@yahoo.com
Tel.: 02 298 6420-23

Al-Mustaqbal Hospital
Nablus St (near the Dutch Rep. Office)
Al-Bireh | Tel.: 02 240 4562-4

Red Crescent Hospital
5 Hilal St, Al-Bireh
birehrc@palnet.com
Tel.: 02 240 6260/6270

PRACTICAL TIPS

HOSPITALS IN BETHLEHEM
Caritas Baby Hospital
cbheld@netvision.net.il
Tel.: 02 275 8500

HOSPITALS IN NABLUS
Nablus Specialty Hospital
Omar Bin Alkhattab st. – Najah University St.
Tel: +970 9 2341 501-2-3-4-5
Email: info@nsh-pal.ps

HOSPITALS IN JERUSALEM

In case of serious emergencies, Hadassah Hospital in Ein Kerem, near Jerusalem, has a good reputation. One of the guidebook authors even had surgery there for a broken ankle! Note that access is complicated for Palestinians.

Hadassah Hospital
Ein Kerem
Tel: 02 677 7111
www.hadassah-med.com

Augusta Victoria Hospital
Mount of Olives
info@avh.org
Tel.: 02 627 9911

Al-Maqassed Hospital
Mount of Olives
mak.hospa.@p-ol.co
Tel.: 02 627 0222 x 9

St. Joseph Hospital
Nashashibi St, Sheikh Jarrah
info@stjoseph.cc
Tel.: 02 591 1911

WHERE TO STAY IN RAMALLAH
Ramallah boasts many overnight options to suit different budgets. These are a few of our recommendations.

$ **Hostel in Ramallah**
(℡ 02-296-3555 | www.hostelinramallah.com)
Located 1.16 km from the city center
This quirky hostel, a five-minute walk from Yasser Arafat Square, is spread over three floors of an apartment building, with a half-dozen dorms and a range of single and double rooms. Staffed by a rotating cast of international volunteers, it has one of the best roof terraces in the city.

$ **Area D Hostel**
(℡ 056 934-9042 | www.ramallahhostel.com)
Located 0.77 km from the city center
Area D is one of only a handful of international standard hostels in the West Bank. Its spotless dorms and double rooms are basic, but the shared lounge is a great place to relax, meet other travelers, and plan excursions.

$$ **Royal Court Hotel**
(℡ 02-296-4040 | www.rcshotel.com)
Located 1.42 km from the city center
This centrally-located boutique hotel is modern, hip, and reliable. Many of the rooms come with kitchen facilities and balconies, and all have good wifi. The owner is a climber (same owner as Vintage Cafe, which is located on the ground floor).

PRACTICAL TIPS

$$$ Millennium Hotel
(© 02-298-5888)
Located 1.13 km from the city center
Formerly the Mövenpick (and still referred to as such by taxi drivers), the Millennium is probably Ramallah's most upscale hotel and the go-to place for business travelers. The hotel features huge rooms, excellent staff, and great facilities, including a gym and pool (summer only).

0 $ **At the house of a friendly climber**
There are always climbers who love to host. Just start asking around at Wadi Climbing Gym or on one of their trips.

WHERE AND WHAT TO EAT IN RAMALLAH
Ramallah has a growing reputation as a cosmopolitan city with plenty of good restaurants. These are a few of our favorites.

Breakfast
$ **Waleed Restaurant**
Located inside the fruit and vegetable market, this one-time favorite restaurant of Yasser Arafat offers hummus, falafel, aja (omlette), and other classic breakfast items.

$ **Bandali Hummus**
Located in the Old City down the street from the gas station, this is a favorite hummus spot for many locals. Hummus is considered mainly a breakfast food by the way!

$$ **Tarweea Restaurant**
Located in the Old City on the main Rukab Street offering a wide selection of breakfast and lunch items.

Lunch/Dinner
$$ **3Ramallah**
The best budget restaurant in Ramallah! Offers homestyle Palestinian meals in a hip setting.

$$ **Samer Restaurant**
You may need to take a taxi to Samer Restaurant since it is a bit far from the city center. The food is local and delicious, and there are tons of options. This is more of a lunch spot as it closes relatively early.

$$$ **Vintage Café**
Vintage is a new, hip, Western restaurant and coffee shop. They serve breakfast, lunch, and dinner and offer sushi nights and live music on certain days. The owner happens to be a dedicated climber himself.

$$$ **Angelos**
Angelos was the first Western-style restaurant to open in Ramallah back in the 1980s. It serves pizza and pasta if you need to carb load for your climb the next day! Located on Rukab Street, about a 5-minute walk from the Lion Circle/Manara square.

Dessert
$ **Al-Omara Kunafa**
Located directly downtown near Duar Al-Sa'a (Arafat circle/Clock square), this sweet shop serves up local treats including the famous, must-try "Kunafa". Kunafa is a sort of Palestinian cheesecake that originated in Nablus but is famous throughout the Arab world.

$$ **Rukab or Baladna Ice Cream Shops**
These competing ice cream parlors are both located on Rukab Street within walking distance of one another. Their unique, Arabic-style ice cream has been featured in lots of news outlets all over the world.

OUT OF TOWN
If you are traveling out of Ramallah, there are a couple of eating spots in the villages around Ramallah that are worth the trip. Here are a few!

$ **Falafel Republic**
Falafel Republic is small family-run restaurant in the old town of Birzeit, 15 minutes north of Ramallah. It serves some of the best food you can find in restaurants and has achieved absolute cult status.

$$ **Al-Falaha**
Al- Falaha specializes in a traditional Palestinian meal called "Musakhan," which is local bread baked with tons of onions and sumac spice and served with or without chicken on top. You won't be able to get this in many places unless you are invited to a private home! Located in Ein Arik Village about 15 minutes from Ramallah.

$$ **Tabash**
Beautiful outdoor venue located in the village of Jifna (on your way if you are returning from climbing in Yabrud to Ramallah). Tabash is famous for its grilled chicken and a la carte side dishes.

Kunafa at the famous *Al Aqsa* kunafa shop in Nablus' Old City
Photo by Marion Ponserre

PRACTICAL TIPS

$$ **Peter's Place**
This incredible restaurant offers views of the Jordan Valley and delicious, home-cooked meals. Located in Taybeh village, it is the perfect place to stop after a tour of Palestine's famous Taybeh Brewery. Call the restaurant ahead and confirm because their opening schedule can be unpredictable!

WHERE TO GET A DRINK IN RAMALLAH
Ramallah has a unique night life and you will find many bars around town. Here is a sampling of notable options.

$$$ **Snobar**
(Open from April to October): A true refuge from the summer heat and the buzzing city. In the summer, Snobar is popular among climbers to go for a morning climb in Yabrud, relax for some hours at Snobar during the midday heat, then continue with an afternoon climb in Ein Qiniya. Although it is a bit pricey, it is totally worth a visit. (The juice pitchers are a bargain.)

$$ **Garage**
Garage is the most popular bar in Ramallah at the time of writing. You will find it busy most days of the week, and the food is awesome (try the toast salad)!

$ **La Grotta**
Other bars come and go, but La Grotta was always there and will always be there for you when you need it. As the name suggests, it is situated in an old Palestinian building with a vault structure. Shadi, the owner of La Grotta, often plays guitar there, and occasionally you get to hear some artists who still master traditional Palestinian instruments like the Oud.

$$ **Radio (Beit Anise)**
Inhabiting an old house (previously owned by a woman named Anise), Beit Anise is one of the hottest night life spots in the West Bank. You will find it packed on weekend nights in the summer.

WHERE TO SHOP IN RAMALLAH
Grocery shopping in Palestine is a cultural experience in and of itself. The delicious seasonal produce will power your climbing days. Come for the climbing, stay for the pomegranates.

The "Hisba" (local market)
At the Hisba you will find a great variety of vegetables and fruits at cheap prices. Additionally, you will get the full experience of an Arab market, including narrow bustling walkways, excessive haggling, and friendly vendors.

Saleh Khalaf
Saleh Khalaf is the best place to stock up on healthy snacks for your climbing days. It features a large selection of nuts and dried fruits, as well as lots of different spices to bring home with you.

Maxmar
If you ever crave Western food or non-pita bread, Maxmar will provide you refuge with its selection of local and international products.

PRACTICAL TIPS

WHAT TO DO ON REST DAYS
As this is a climbing guidebook, we will only briefly mention a few sightseeing highlights and indicate where to look for further information.

Hiking
Wadi Qelt, Wadi Auja, and Wadi Mukalluk are three popular hikes that we recommend, but there are countless options in the West Bank. Consider picking up a copy of "Walking Palestine" (Szepesi 2012). There are also a number of organizations that plan group hikes on a weekly basis. Check out the Sea Level Bedouin community; they offer hiking trips and overnight camping experiences (contact Jameel: +970568492924 or +970597011708). You can also contact the "Hike Palestine" group on Facebook. Check out the hiking app "Rihleh," featuring a range of below-the-radar hiking trails.

Dead Sea
A classic tourist destination for a reason! The healing waters of the Dead Sea will cure your climbing ailments in no time. The Dead Sea can be visited year-round and is accessible from Jericho by taxi.

Nablus
This northern West Bank city is situated between two mountains and has history dating back thousands of years. Explore the Old City and its markets, visit the old Turkish Baths (separate times for women and men), and eat the hometown dessert staples "kunafa" or "kolaj." Most importantly it also features a newly-developed cliff! (see chapter 9).

Jerusalem
You can't visit Palestine without spending at least some time in this fascinating and complex city. You might want to pick up a tourist guidebook...

Bethlehem
Not only is Bethlehem home to history of biblical proportions, but it also features a few modern attractions. Check out graffiti artist Banksy's "Walled Off Hotel"—a museum, art exhibition, and functioning hotel. Bethlehem is also host to the annual Palestine Marathon, which is an impressive event if you are in town in March. If you go, you must eat and maybe camp at the Hosh El Yasmine organic farm, accessible from town by taxi. Stop by the Visit Palestine Center for tourist information and crafts by local artisans.

Political Tours
There is no better way to understand the political situation than to join a tour of some of the most controversial areas of the West Bank. We recommend any **Green Olive Tour** or the **Breaking the Silence** tour of Hebron.

OTHER INTERESTING THINGS AND PLACES TO SEE:
- **Sebastia village**
- **Jericho** (largest city in the Jordan Valley close to the Dead Sea, on the way to and from Jordan)
- **Jizr Az Zarqa village** (Palestinian fishing village on the coast in Israel)
- **The Golan Heights**
- **Yasser Arafat Tomb and Museum** (Ramallah)

Wadi Climbing Gym
Photo by Tim Bruns

WADI CLIMBING GYM

☏ 059 581 0314*
www.facebook.com/wadiclimbing
www.instagram.com/wadi_climbing
GPS location: 31.886423, 35.22303

Wadi Climbing is the first indoor rock climbing gym in Palestine. Opened in 2016, the gym features boulders, a slack line, and all the necessary climbing training facilities. A day pass costs 30 NIS and shoes/chalk are available for rent.

Wadi Climbing also offers outdoor gear rentals of shoes, harnesses, helmets, and bouldering pads. A smaller bouldering gym, established by the Palestine Club for Mountain Sports (PAMSD), opened in Bethlehem in 2017. Wadi Climbing gym is located in the basement of Trifitness Health Club (just off the main Jerusalem road) and is accessible either by taxi (15 NIS) or by shared taxi (called "service" pronounced sair-vees) from downtown; ask for the service to Satah Marhaba. The service taxis park and wait for passengers on a street corner that is a five-minute walk from Al Manara circle. The GPS location of where they wait is 31.901965, 35.209068. Ask the driver to be dropped at Trifitness.

On weekends, Wadi Climbing offers guided outdoor climbing trips to locations near Ramallah. Even if you are an experienced climber, these trips are a fun social event and way to meet locals!

Keep up to date on the Wadi Climbing Facebook and Instagram pages!

*Phone number subject to change based on current management

NATURE AND GEOLOGY
By Christelle Bakhache

GEOLOGY

The West Bank is largely dominated by a range of low mountains on the western side of the Jordan Valley, and is characterized by an arid to semi-arid landscape of hills and valleys. Within a relatively small area, altitude ranges between 400 meters below sea level to 950 meters above sea level. Thus, the climate varies widely. While the higher altitudes get relatively high levels of rainfall (about 600mm p.a., though mostly concentrated in the winter months), conditions in the lower Jordan Valley are arid with low levels of rainfall (150mm p.a.). This hilltop runoff rainwater was responsible for the formation of the "wadis" (Arabic for valley), which go down into the Jordan Valley and make for some of the best climbing spots in the region. The rocks are mainly composed of marine sediments (limestone and dolomite).

As part of the Great Rift Valley, the Jordan Valley marks the fault line between the Eurasian and the Arabian tectonic plates. Further down in the Jordan Valley sedimentary and magmatic rock layers are preserved in continuous sequences. The outcropping formations of rock around the lower parts are characterized by alternating deposition and erosion phases—not the best rock climbing material. Apart from Wadi Tamer, all climbing areas are therefore in the higher parts of the wadis and around the hilltops of the West Bank.

Most of the climbing areas feature solid limestone similar to Mediterranean crags in Italy, France, and Spain. The rock quality of the crags featured in this guidebook is usually very good, although you sometimes have to climb the first two or three meters across loose marlstone until you reach solid limestone.

Most of the porous rock in the mountainous land of the West Bank permits rainwater to percolate and creates resurgence that keeps the rock wet after heavy rainfalls. Nevertheless, the sunny and dry climate of the region helps the rock to dry quickly.

The Great West Bank Aquifer is the main ground water basin in the region, significantly at stake in the conflict over the scarce water resources between Israel and Palestine.

Anas Askar enjoying "The Pearl," 6b (page 79) in New Ein Qiniya.
Photo by Markus Maier

NATURE AND GEOLOGY

Rock Hyrax
Photo by Dario Franchetti

FLORA

Climbing in Palestine offers plenty of opportunities to observe native plants and animals. Over the seasons, the landscape tends to vary from high floral diversity in spring to burnt meadows at the end of summer. The thin topsoil layer, especially around limestone aquifers, makes for a bushy vegetation of low-lying trees and herbaceous plants (including spiky ones such as the widespread Sarcopterium—beware!). This trend is reinforced by the long-practiced tradition of goat and sheep grazing, which results in herbaceous and bushy plants rather than trees of higher growth.

Aromatic plants, often used for cooking in the Middle East, such as Maramia (sage), Na'ana (mint) and Za'atar (wild thyme) grow and perfume the air all year long. They are a great addition to your tea after a climbing session and are traditionally harvested from the hills by locals. A few higher trees, characteristic of both the landscape and the culture of the region, can also be found. Carob trees produce pods that are used in local cuisine.

Olive trees, a symbol of Palestine, are the source of precious olive fruits and oil. The old Ottoman law, still recognized in Palestine, makes the olive tree even more important as its presence can be enough to prevent expropriation. The underlying principle to this is that the presence of an olive tree proves continuous cultivation of the land and prevents it from being declared Israeli state land. Consequently there have been frequent occurances of olive trees being uprooted or destroyed by Israeli settlers in attempt to lay claim to land in the West Bank.

NATURE AND GEOLOGY

FAUNA

Kestrels, tortoises, rock hyraxes, gazelles, wild boars, jackals, scorpions, and snakes have all been spotted around Palestine's climbing crags. Most commonly-spotted is the Mediterranean Spur-Thighed tortoise (*Testuda graeca ibera*, picture below), which can be seen soaking up the sun on warm days after rain. The vast majority of snakes found in Palestine are harmless and perform a public service by eating rodents and insects. That being said, climbers have spotted Palestinian Vipers (*Viper Palaestinae*) in some of the climbing areas. This snake is venomous with a dangerous (but rarely fatal) bite. Additionally, the cliffs are home to a number of lizards, which are harmless but like to hide in the comfortable pockets and jugs of climbing routes!

Rock hyraxes are a common sight in the bigger valleys of Palestine. In Ein Fara and some other areas, gazelles can be observed frequently. The shy jackals, however, are very rarely spotted, but their shrill call can often be heard at dusk and dawn. Palestine's wild boar population is surprisingly large, and it even continues to grow. There are hardly any natural predators for the boars, and for religious and cultural reasons, neither Muslims nor Jews are particularly keen on hunting them. Boars enjoy the remoteness of some of the climbing crags and can sometimes be spotted resting in caves. Normally, you only see the remnants of their search for food; they dig up patches of earth. Encounters between wild boars and climbers are usually mutually shocking and result in the boar fleeing hastily. Caution is advised in spring when female wild boars are protective of the newborn piglets.

The surroundings of all crags covered in this book are used by Bedouin to graze their herds. You will most likely encounter some curious goat trying to taste your delicious-looking climbing rope.

Tortoise with offspring
Photo by Dario Franchetti

NATURE AND GEOLOGY

CONSERVATION AND SUSTAINABILITY IN PALESTINE

Nature reserves exist in the West Bank but are divided according to the Oslo Areas (A, B, C). Israel has created controversial nature reserves in some of the most beautiful parts of Area C. The Palestinian Authority is responsible for some nature reserves in Areas A and B. These reserves fall under the joint responsibility of the Palestinian Environmental Authority and the Palestinian Ministry of Agriculture. The establishment of the nature reserves in Area A has already diminished environmentally harmful behavior such as unofficial dumping of waste.

Most of the climbing spots featured in this book, even though located on patches of land that do not have agricultural purposes, have no particular status of protection. Some unfortunate precedents exist in treating these areas as dumpsites, and the general problem of littering does not spare the crags. The authors of this book as well as the broader climbing community have participated in keeping the area clean; picking up their own trash and any trash found on the spot. Follow the lead and please be respectful of the environment when climbing.

If you are interested in learning more about the local fauna and flora and the environment, you can get more information from the Palestine Museum of Natural History or visit www.mahmiyat.ps, which gives a great overview of protected areas and nature in Palestine.

Flowers in spring, Yabrud. Photo by Markus Maier

01 . YABRUD ★★★★

01 YABRUD

Routes	56
Length	12-20m
Rock	Limestone
Political Area	B
Coordinates	31.9830840N, 35.2404560E

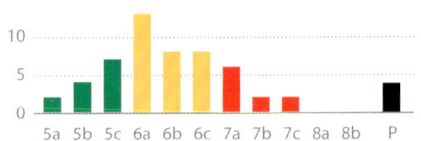

OVERVIEW
Only 20 minutes from Ramallah, Yabrud has become the most prominent crag in the Ramallah area. It now features 56 sport climbing routes on superb limestone. It was first developed by Tim Bruns, Will Harris, Dario Franchetti, and Kim Van Der Putten, but over the years many foreigners and Palestinians have contributed routes to this amazing crag.

SEASON
The Yabrud cliffs face south, which makes it an ideal climbing location in the late fall, winter, and early spring but very hot in the summer. In the summer, the crag is in the shade until 11:00 am, thus it is recommended to climb in the early morning. The best months of the year are November/December and March/April. January and February can be great months, but the climbing days are limited due to rain and occasional snow.

Christelle Bakhache going lightly, just before crux on "Holly Go Lightly," 6c+ (page 40)
Photo by Markus Maier

GEAR
All the routes at Yabrud are pure sport and are equipped with an anchor station with rappel ring. Most routes range from 4 to 8 bolts long. A standard 60-meter rope will be plenty (and possibly even enough for two routes at once). Sun protection is a must!

YABRUD

DIRECTIONS

The trip to the Yabrud cliffs takes about 20 minutes by car from Ramallah, with two main driving routes depending on whether the road next to the Beit El Settlement is open. There is also the option to reach the climbing site by public transport:

Option 1 (if the road is open): From Al-Manara circle in Ramallah, drive northeast on Ersal Street towards Bir Zeit for about 4 km. Take a slight right onto route 463 and drive 1km. Take a left on route 466 (the old Nablus road) and drive 3.6 km north past the Beit El settlement on your right and Jalazun camp on your left. Continue for 7 km down into the valley past Dura El Qari'a village on your right and Ein Sinya village on your left. At the bottom of the valley, take a right onto a dirt road that heads up a valley to the right. You will see the cliff band ahead of you up the valley. Park your car anywhere alongside the dirt road and walk all the way up the dirt road until you are at the same height as the bottom of the cliffs, then hike north to reach the climbing routes. Most recently (January 2018), a barricade of rubble has been erected at the beginning of the dirt road to prevent illegal garbage dumping. You can either park in front of the barricade

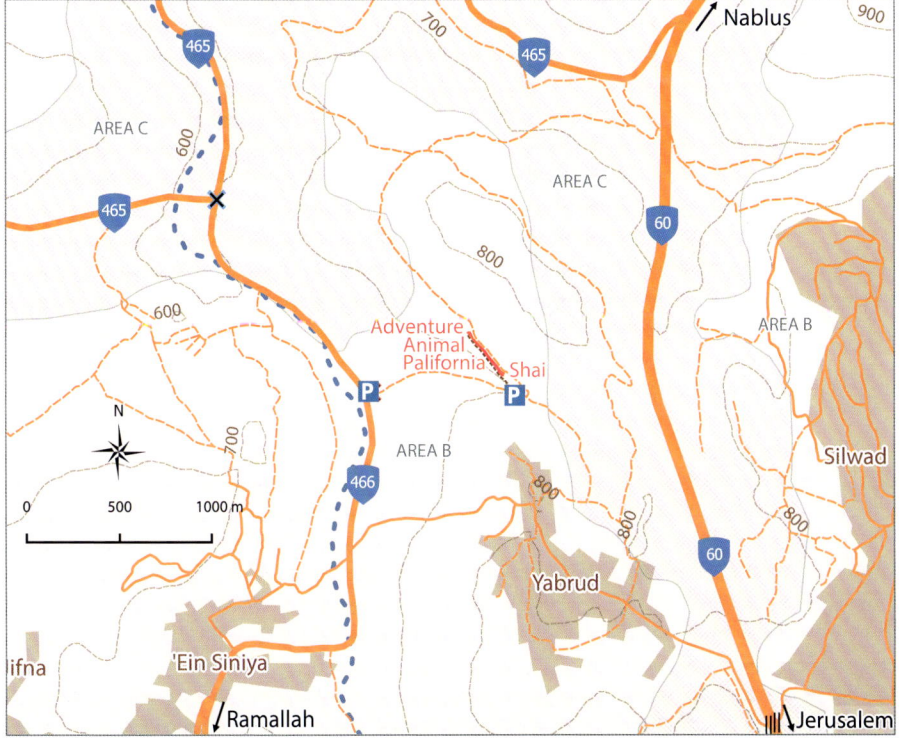

YABRUD

Wahid Masri and Amer Kurdi enjoying tea in Yabrud. Photo by Tim Bruns

and hike a bit further, or you can take a longer detour to the actual village of Yabrud and approach the cliff from the top of the hill.

Option 2 (if the road is closed): From Al-Manara circle in Ramallah drive northeast on Ersal Street towards Bir Zeit for 4 km. Don't turn right onto route 463 but continue on the road for another minute. In Surda, take a right up a steep hill towards the large golden mosque. If the main road is closed, there will be other cars using this route. Take a right at the T intersection and follow the road until it joins the old Nablus road in front of the Beit El settlement. Take a left and drive north past the Beit El settlement on your right and Jalazun camp on your left. From here, follow the directions in Option 1 (above).

Option 3 (public transportation): The Yabrud cliffs can be reached easily and cheaply by "service," the yellow minibuses that are omnipresent in Palestine. The service to Yabrud village can be found in the tunnel directly across the street from the Area D youth hostel near the Jamel Abdul Nasser mosque. This is right next to the station for buses to Jerusalem. The service to Yabrud costs 7 NIS. It runs on weekdays during daylight hours but waits until the bus is full to leave. This can take up to 40 minutes during slow hours. The weekend connections are far less frequent and almost nonexistent on Fridays. Ask the service driver to drop you off on the dirt road just past the small supermarket in Yabrud. You will then follow the dirt road down into the valley and reach the cliffs on your right after a 10-minute walk. At the end of the day, you can a catch a service back to Ramallah in front of the Yabrud supermarket.

YABRUD

PRESERVATION AND ETIQUETTE

Climbers have formed a good relationship with the local Yabrud municipality and gained permission and support for climbing activity at the cliffs. That said, it is vital that visitors perpetuate the good relationship with the local community by being respectful and culturally sensitive.

Leave No Trace: Pack up all trash (including cigarette butts, toilet paper, and even trash that is not yours), follow established trails, and respect flora & fauna.

Cultural sensitivity: Climb with a shirt on; avoid wearing revealing clothes; be friendly and respectful to locals. Feel free to share your harness with locals and give them a chance to climb. They will greatly appreciate it!

HIGHLINING

In 2016, Yabrud was host to the first ever highline in Palestine. The highline rig is about 40 meters long and traverses the valley from north to south over the dirt access road. The site is equipped with five 10mm expansion bolts at either anchor point, but the hangers have been removed. There is a definite "no-fall" zone on the north side of the valley. It is best to walk from the obvious rock protrusion on the southern side of the valley.

CRAG DEVELOPERS

A number of people have contributed to the development of Yabrud as a climbing site. The first developers were Tim Bruns, Will Harris, Dario Franchetti, and Kim Van der Putten. Afterwards, Selim Schweitzer, Benjamin Korff, Camille Dupouy, Andrea Bernardi; Markus Maier and Christelle Bakhache joined their ranks.

Highlining in Yabrud
Photo by Miranda Oakley

YABRUD | SHAI SECTOR

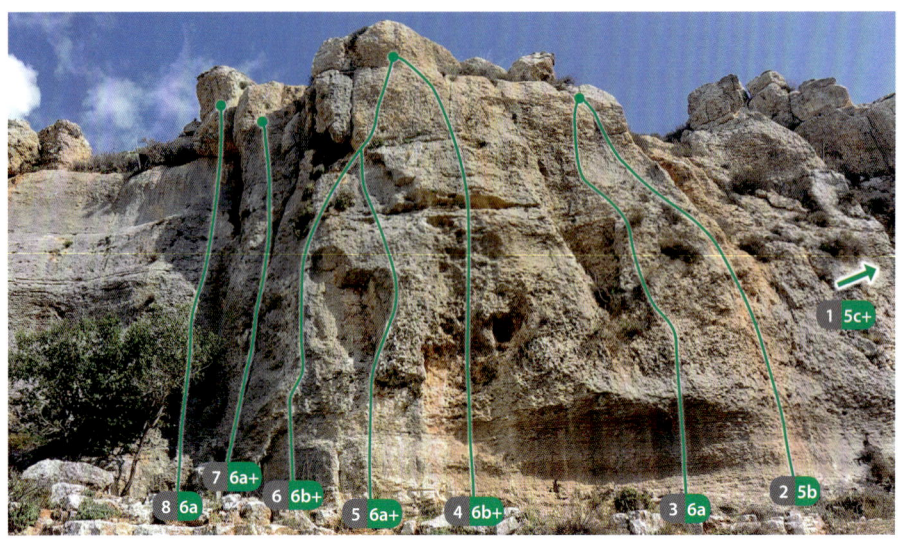

SHAI SECTOR RIGHT This is the first sector when you approach the crag from the parking. It features a good number of lower-grade routes.

ROUTE	GRADE	RATING	METERS	BOLTS	STYLE	DEVELOPED
1 Life on the Edge	5c+	★	10m	4 bolts	Sport	2016
Short route with some tricky moves along the edge.						
2 Criss Cross Hob	5b	★	13m	5 bolts	Sport	2016
Starts on the small balcony, ends on a slab.						
3 Where is the Drill Bit?	6a	★	13m	6 bolts	Sport	2016
Bouldery first move. The guys who bolted this route did not have a very lucky start to their bolting day.						
4 Russian Eagle	6b+	★★	16m	5 bolts	Sport	2015
Start up the steep pockets and reach the crux on the crimps near the top. Reaching the anchor station to the left is tough for short climbers.						
5 Dubke Dance	6a+	★★★	16m	6 bolts	Sport	2015
A difficult move off the ground leads into great laybacking, crimps and more laybacking. A fantastic climb with varied movement!						
6 The Next Century	6b+	★	18m	7 bolts	Sport	2017
Technical and crimpy, shares the anchor station with Dubke Dance. FA by Tawfiq Najada						
7 Nablusi Soap	6a+	★★	15m	5 bolts	Sport	2015
Start behind the tree and move up into the natural crack system.						
8 Baloota	6a	★	16m	5 bolts	Sport	2015
Start all the way behind the baloota tree and pull the roof at the top.						

SHAI SECTOR | YABRUD

SHAI SECTOR MIDDLE

ROUTE	GRADE	RATING	METERS	BOLTS	STYLE	DEVELOPED
9 Bes Sukar	6a	★★	12m	4 bolts	Sport	2015

Clip the first two bolts and make a few difficult, balance-y moves to reach the edge. Cruise through easier terrain to the top.

10 Sukar Ma Shai	5c+	★	11m	3 bolts	Sport	2015

Start below the anchor station and head straight up the slab.

11 Shai Ma Sukar	5c	★	12m	4 bolts	Sport	2015

Start to the left and tiptoe to the right to reach the anchor.

12 Hai Hilalik	5b	★★★	14m	5 bolts	Sport	2015

Beautiful slab for beginners after the more powerful beginning.
Make sure not to miss the crescent moon hold which gives this route its name.

YABRUD | SHAI SECTOR

SHAI SECTOR LEFT

ROUTE	GRADE	RATING	METERS	BOLTS	STYLE	DEVELOPED
13 Ma'arajaat	5c+	★	15m	5 bolts	Sport	2015
A good warm-up with delicate moves and a big pull up at the top.						
14 Maqlooba Dazed	6b	★★	14 m	5 bolts	Sport	2015
Pull on jugs until the exposed face, solve the crux and climb the ridge to end. Careful on the third clip...						
15 The Dark Side of the Sun	6a+	★★	16 m	6 bolts	Sport	2018
After the second bolt traverse left. To avoid rope drag unclip the second quickdraw after you clipped the third one.						
16 Mia fil Mia	7a+	★★	14m	5 bolts	Sport	2016
The 100th route bolted by our team in Palestine! Hard and bouldery start and a slabby ending. Pre-clipping of the first two quickdraws is advised.						

Tawfiq Najada on
"Tannourine Dream," 7b (page 35)
Photo by Philipp Zwehl

YABRUD | PALIFORNIA SECTOR

PALIFORNIA SECTOR | YABRUD

PALIFORNIA SECTOR RIGHT

ROUTE	GRADE	RATING	METERS	BOLTS	STYLE	DEVELOPED
17 Henry's Project	P	P	16m		Sport	2016
"Well, it has got features" was all Tony Yao said about it. No one has been able to do the first ascent yet.						
18 Chris Shawarma, project	P	P	18m	8 bolts	Sport	2015
Email us if you send this beast! Bonus points if you stick the dyno and enjoy a shawarma sandwich on the top after the send!						
19 Goin' Back to Pali Project	P	P	20 m		Sport	2016
Another impossible gift from Tony Yao. Sharp holds and dynamic moves are waiting for a first ascent.						
20 Pickpocket	7b	★★★	19m	7 bolts	Sport	2016
Clip the first draw from the ground. Sustained, difficult, and incredibly fun.						
21 Hard for Today	6a+	★★★	19m	6 bolts	Sport	2015
Beautiful jugs lead to easier climbing.						
22 Palifornia Dreamin'	6a+	★★	20m	7 bolts	Sport	2015
This is the longest route in Yabrud and should not be missed. Be careful when clipping the 2nd bolt.						
23 My Humps	6a+	★	18m	6 bolts	Sport	2015
Similar to Hard for Today, this route is a little more sustained.						
24 Goats Are Cool	7a+	★★	18m	7 bolts	Sport	2015
Crimpy, perfect rock follows the orange streak.						
25 Kaboos (Nightmare), project	P	P	17m	6 bolts	Sport	2016
The moves on the first half of this route have been done... can you figure out the second half?						
26 Tannourine Dream	7b	★★★	18m	5 bolts	Sport	2014
Named after the famous climbing area in Lebanon, this route is truly a dream! Climb the natural line up the tufa and enjoy the crux at the top!						

Nina Caprez on "Tannourine Dream," 7b (page 35)
Photo by Sam Challeat

Ishaq Rajabi on
"Hard for Today," 6a+ (page 35)
Photo by Miranda Oakley

YABRUD | PALIFORNIA SECTOR

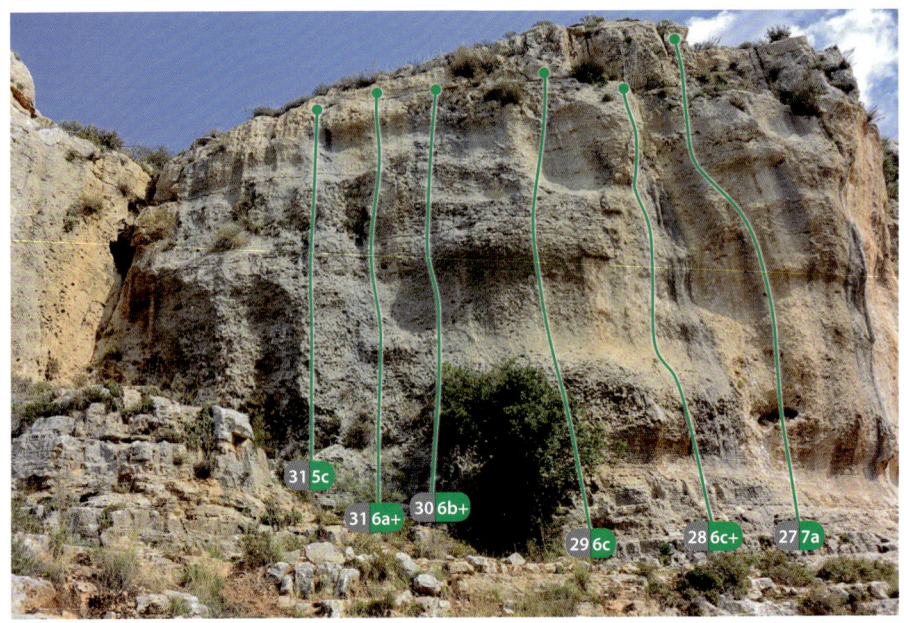

PALIFORNIA SECTOR LEFT

ROUTE	GRADE	RATING	METERS	BOLTS	STYLE	DEVELOPED
27 The Bullet and the Feather	7a	★★★	19m	6 bolts	Sport	2015
Follow the route through the hole to the overhanging face above. The anchor is high.						
28 Goat Face Killa	6c+	★★	16m	6 bolts	Sport	2016
Crimpy and sustained climb. Sharp but great fun.						
29 One Move to 7th Heaven	6c	★	16m	5 bolts	Sport	2016
Hard crux, the rest of the route is 6b. The name is slightly misleading. Maybe Tim had the UIAA grading scale in mind.						
30 Viper Palaestinae	6b+	★★	15m	6 bolts	Sport	2016
Start up the seemingly blank face and hold on as the route gets steeper and steeper!						
31 Ripped Pants	6a+	★★	15m	5 bolts	Sport	2016
The first route bolted by a Palestinian team.						
32 Now You See Me, Now You Don't	5c	★	13m	5 bolts	Sport	2016
Varied movement on great rock.						

ANIMAL KINGDOM SECTOR | YABRUD

ANIMAL KINGDOM SECTOR RIGHT

ROUTE	GRADE	RATING	METERS	BOLTS	STYLE	DEVELOPED
33 Qalandia Crimper	6c+|7a	★★	13m	4 bolts	Sport	2014
Prepare for merciless crimps and desperate moves.						
34 Za'atar	5b	★	13m	4 bolts	Sport	2014
The first route that was bolted in Yabrud.						
35 Nell and Oriol	6b	★★	15m	5 bolts	Sport	2016
Start in front of the small cave and keep climbing slightly to the right.						

YABRUD | ANIMAL KINGDOM SECTOR

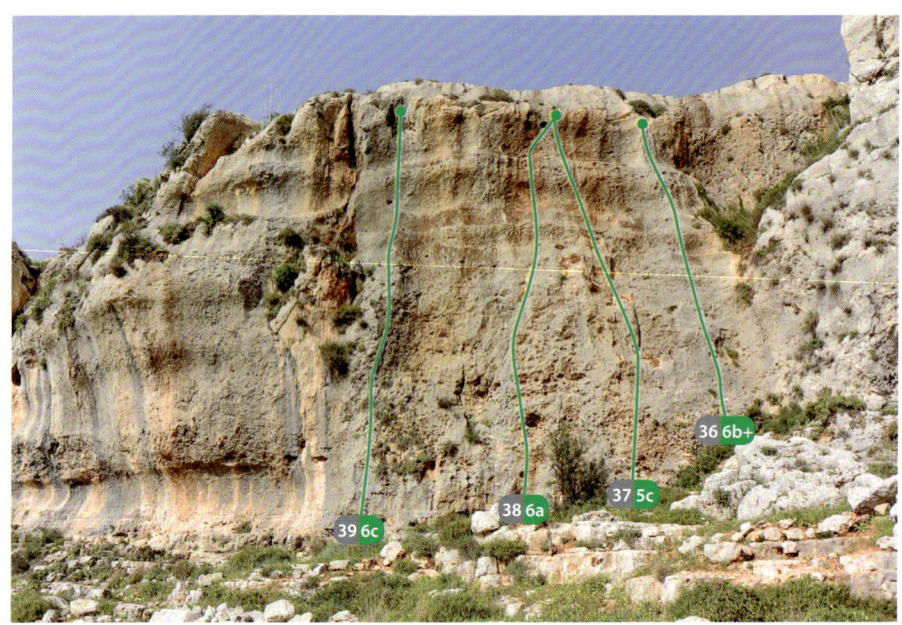

ANIMAL KINGDOM SECTOR MIDDLE

ROUTE	GRADE	RATING	METERS	BOLTS	STYLE	DEVELOPED
36 Half an Avocado	6b+	★★	17m	6 bolts	Sport	2018
Technical and slabby climbing. Don't offer to share your food if you only have half an avocado!						
37 Hofra One	5c	★	16m	5 bolts	Sport	2015
Start to the right of the bush and climb some dirty rock to reach the delicate crux at the top.						
38 Hofra Two	6a	★	16m	5 bolts	Sport	2015
Aim for the hole (hofra) at the top!						
39 Holly Go Lightly	6c	★★★	17m	6 bolts	Sport	2016
Technical and balance-y climb. Great fun! Go lightly on that crux!						

ANIMAL KINGDOM SECTOR | YABRUD

ANIMAL KINGDOM SECTOR MIDDLE II

ROUTE	GRADE	RATING	METERS	BOLTS	STYLE	DEVELOPED
40 Le Visionnaire	6a+	★★	14m	4 bolts	Sport	2016

A nice climb on the wonderfully solid rock that Yabrud is famous for.

41 Thoma wa Basal	5c+	★	14m	5 bolts	Sport	2015

Start in the corner and follow the route to the tufa feature at the top.

42 Walk the Line	5b	★★	16m	6 bolts	Sport	2016

Climb along the arête and follow the obvious line.

YABRUD | ANIMAL KINGDOM SECTOR

ANIMAL KINGDOM SECTOR LEFT

ROUTE	GRADE	RATING	METERS	BOLTS	STYLE	DEVELOPED
43 Solhafa's Shell	6b+	★	16m	6 bolts	Sport	2015
Climb to the roof and solve the balance-y crux to gain the ledge. Make sure your belayer is close to the wall and with you until you clip the 3rd bolt.						
44 The Thief's Road	7a	★	16m	5 bolts	Sport	2015
6b climbing until the tippy top...						
45 Adamantium	5a	★★★	16m	6 bolts	Sport	2015
Fun slab climbing on the face to the left of the crack. Named after the impenetrable limestone of Yabrud. A must-do route.						
46 Diamond Mine	6c	★	17m	5 bolts	Sport	2016
Start standing on a pile of rocks. The first hold is really high up.						

ADVENTURE SECTOR | YABRUD

ADVENTURE SECTOR RIGHT

ROUTE	GRADE	RATING	METERS	BOLTS	STYLE	DEVELOPED
47 Avada Kadabra	7a	★★	18m	6 bolts	Sport	2016
This shares the first bolt with Sahalia (Lizard). Campus up the big holds then traverse right. Big moves and small crimps are the name of the game!						
48 Sahalia (Lizard)	6c	★★	18m	6 bolts	Sport	2016
It might be easier to campus the first few moves...						
49 Palestinian White Boy	7c	★★	11 m	5 bolts	Sport	2016
Hard boulder problem, FA by Tyler Myers						

YABRUD | ADVENTURE SECTOR

ADVENTURE SECTOR LEFT

ROUTE	GRADE	RATING	METERS	BOLTS	STYLE	DEVELOPED
50 Alternative Facts	6c+	★★★	19m	7bolts	Sport	2017
After the pigeon hole continue right.						
51 One Flew Over the Cuckoo's Nest	7a+	★★★	19m	5 bolts	Sport	2017
Incredible moves are waiting for those who dare to climb past the pigeon excrement in the beginning.						
52 Feige Dattel (Cowardly Date)	7c+	★★	19m	7 bolts	Sport	2019
Don't be a coward and move past the fifth bolt before you clip. Shares anchor and last bolt with 51.						
53 Adventure Time	6c	★★★	18m	6 bolts	Sport	2016
This route features unique climbing in a pumpy style that is not common in Yabrud.						
54 Land of Ooo	6b	★★	18m	6 bolts	Sport	2016
Be tall for the first move...						
55 Circus Show	6a	★	12m	5 bolts	Sport	2017
After all, Ewa got her circus show.						
56 Princess Bubblegum	4+	★	17m	4 bolts	Sport	2016
A good climb for first-timers.						

Miranda Oakley on "Maqlooba Dazed," 6b (page 32)
Photo by Julie Ellison

Madaleine Sorkin on
"The Bullet and the Feather," 7a (page 38)
Photo by Henna Taylor

Mohammed "Abu Sayyaf"
Najada making tea
Photo by Henna Taylor

Anas Askar on "Viper Palaestinae," 6b+ (page 38)
Photo by Ray Wood

02 . EIN YABRUD ★★☆☆☆

02 EIN YABRUD

Routes	22
Length	12-25m
Rock	Limestone
Political Area	C
Coordinates	31.947545, 35.243317

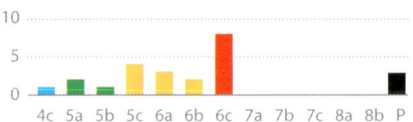

OVERVIEW
Ein Yabrud is the least visited of the locations bolted by the authors and local Palestinian climbers, but that is not to say there are not fantastic routes! The Castle sector is truly unique and offers limestone that is unlike any you will find elsewhere in Palestine. There are some gems here and it is worth a visit.

Access road to
Ein Yabrud climbing area
Photo by Tim Bruns

SEASON
The cliffs in Ein Yabrud face northwest. Often the valley can be cooler than Yabrud and a better destination for hot days. Like all locations in Palestine, the best seasons are from fall to spring.

GEAR
All but one of the climbs in Ein Yabrud are sport climbs equipped with bolts and anchor stations with rappelling rings. Ten quickdraws and a 60 meter rope are sufficient for all of the routes.

EIN YABRUD

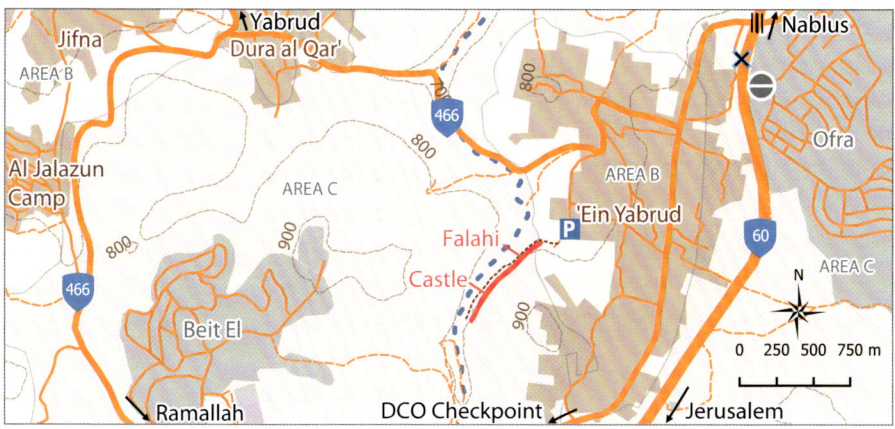

DIRECTIONS

The trip takes about 20 minutes by car from Ramallah. There are two ways to get to the location by car from Ramallah depending on whether or not the road next to the Beit El settlement is open.

Option 1 (if the road is open): From Al-Manara circle in Ramallah, drive northeast on Ersal Street towards Bir Zeit for about 4 km. Take a slight right onto route 463 and drive 1 km. Take a left on route 466 (the old Nablus road) and drive 3.6 km north past the Beit El settlement on your right and Jalazun camp on your left. When you reach the intersection at the Dura El Qari'a village take a right, pass through the village and follow the winding road through the valley. After roughly 2.5 km, you will pass a school on your right and come to a sharp left turn in the road that leads to Ein Yabrud village. Take a right here and follow the road past large houses until the asphalt ends and a dirt road continues. Follow the dirt road for about 100 meters and park the car. Accessing the cliff is a little tricky since there is no trail. Hike west from the car and slightly down into the valley to access the cliffs from the north end.

Option 2 (if the road is closed): From Al-Manara circle in Ramallah, drive northeast on Ersal Street towards Bir Zeit for 4 km. Don't turn right onto route 463, but continue on the road for another minute. In Surda, take a right up a steep hill towards the large golden mosque. If the main road is closed, there will be other cars using this route. Take a right at the T intersection and follow the road until it joins the old Nablus road in front of the Beit El settlement. Take a left and drive north past the Beit El settlement on your right and Jalazun camp on your left. From here, follow the directions in Option 1 (above).

Option 3 (public transportation): The Ein Yabrud cliffs can be reached easily and cheaply by "service," the yellow minibuses that are omnipresent in Palestine. The service to Ein Yabrud village can be found in the tunnel directly across the street from the Area D youth hostel near the Jamel Abdul Nasser

EIN YABRUD

mosque. This is right next to the station for buses to Jerusalem. The service to Ein Yabrud costs about 7 NIS. It runs on weekdays during daylight hours but waits until the bus is full to leave. This can take up to 40 minutes during slow hours. The weekend connections are far less frequent and almost non-existent on Fridays. Ask the service driver to drop you at the school before the first curve when entering the village. Follow the description above (Option 1) to reach the crag.

Spring in Ein Yabrud
Photo by Markus Maier

PRESERVATION AND ETIQUETTE

Climbers have formed a good relationship with the local Ein Yabrud municipality and gained permission and support for climbing activity at the cliffs. That said, it is vital that visitors perpetuate the good relationship with the local community by being respectful and culturally sensitive. Ein Yabrud features beautiful views and is rarely visited unless by climbers. Occasionally you will meet curious local villagers. Please uphold the following values while enjoying the area.

Leave No Trace: Pack out all trash (including cigarette butts and toilet paper), follow established trails, respect flora & fauna, and even pick up trash that's not yours.

Cultural sensitivity: Climb with a shirt on, avoid wearing revealing clothes, be friendly and respectful to locals. Feel free to share your harness with locals and give them a chance to climb. They will greatly appreciate it!

EIN YABRUD

CONFLICT

One concern about Ein Yabrud is its proximity to the Beit El settlement. Armed settlers and Israeli soldiers have been encountered in the valley, which can be uncomfortable but this has not caused any further problems thus far. Most recently there were reports that some settlers from Beit El started to come to the Ein Yabrud cliff to climb. In most cases those settlers are armed, so take care to not get into any fights, especially if you are Palestinian and there are no foreign climbers around. Palestinian climbers and foreigners used to camp at the base of this cliff, but the campfire attracted the Israeli army and the campers were told to leave.

Inas Radaydeh on "The First Cut is the Deepest," 6a (page 55)
Photo by Markus Maier

EIN YABRUD | FALAHI SECTOR

FALAHI SECTOR This is the first sector when you approach the crag from the parking area.

ROUTE	GRADE	RATING	METERS	BOLTS	STYLE	DEVELOPED
1 The Goat's Hairdresser	5c+	★	17m	5 bolts	Sport	2015

Enjoy this stemming and don't forget about the roof above! A nice warm up for the Ein Yabrud style of climbing.

2 Ballerina	6c	★★	17m	5 bolts	Sport	2015

Technical middle section requires problem solving skills.

3 Matthew's Bush	6a+	★	17m	5 bolts	Sport	2016

It gets its grade for the last move onto the ledge. Named after the bold and fearless Matt who made this route what it is.

4 Foxy Lady	6b+	★	18m	5 bolts	Sport	2015

Shallow pockets and tiny flakes. Sustained.

5 Unnamed project	P	P	20m	6 bolts	Sport	2015

Enjoy this long and hard route, let us know if you get the first ascent!

CASTLE SECTOR | EIN YABRUD

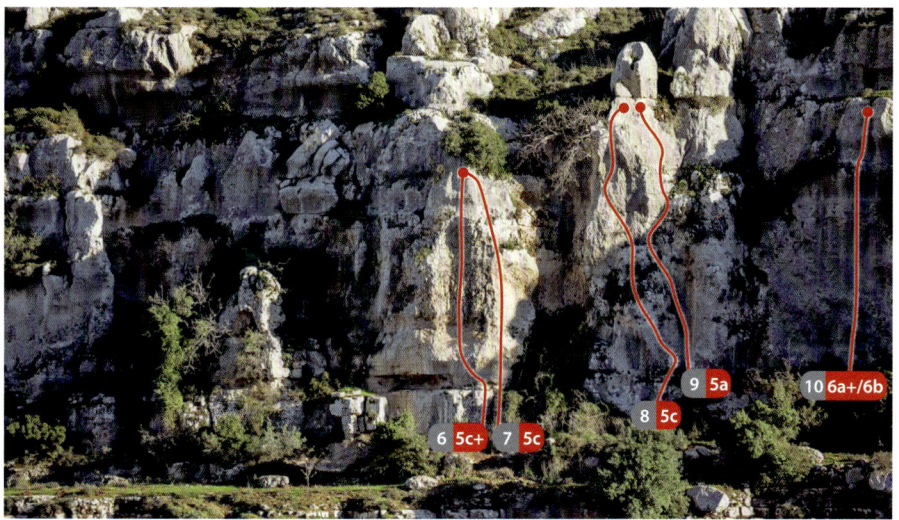

CASTLE SECTOR LEFT
The walk between the two sectors is about 5 minutes long and can be overgrown with wild brush.

ROUTE	GRADE	RATING	METERS	BOLTS	STYLE	DEVELOPED
6 The Game of Thorns	5c+	★	13m	4 bolts	Sport	2015
Very sharp rock forces you to climb delicately.						
7 Prickly Pear	5c	★	13m	4 bolts	Sport	2015
Sharp. Shares an anchor station with The Game of Thorns.						
8 On the Edge	5c	★	15m	5 bolts	Sport	2019
Gets harder at the end and has a great escape.						
9 Bergsteiger	5a	★	15m	5 bolts	Sport	2019
10 Neat and Petite	6a+/6b	★	15m	6 bolts	Sport	2018
If climbed straight it's 6b. If you go right to the big holes it's 6a+.						

EIN YABRUD | CASTLE SECTOR

CASTLE SECTOR RIGHT

ROUTE	GRADE	RATING	METERS	BOLTS	STYLE	DEVELOPED
11 Al-Qala'a (The Fortress)	6c+	★★★	21m	10 bolts	Sport	2015

The longest route in Ein Yabrud. Have fun storming the castle!

12 A Friend from Down Unda'	4+	★	13m	6 bolts	Sport	2015

Named for an Australian with a fear of heights. Careful when lowering to avoid the tree.

13 Three Month Fling	6b+	★★	17m	6 bolts	Sport	2015

It's like climbing three boulder problems stacked on top of each other.

14 Selim the Boar Hunter	6c+	★★	17m	6 bolts	Sport	2015

Similar to Three Month Fling, this route features three boulder problems with rests in between.

15 This Week in Palestine	6c+	★★★	18m	7 bolts	Sport	2015

Scenic climbing up the exposed corner.

CASTLE SECTOR | EIN YABRUD

ROUTE	GRADE	RATING	METERS	BOLTS	STYLE	DEVELOPED
16 Gandalf's Eagle	6c	★★★	16m	6 bolts	Sport	2015

A beautiful route on solid rock. Pretty much slopers all the way up! It ends at two bolts.

Gandalf's Eagle Extension project (16)	P	P	19m	0 bolts	Sport	2015

Continue past the two bolts of Gandalf's Eagle and you will reach an anchor station. The route gets steep and the holds disappear.

17 The Accent	6a+	★★★	16m	6 bolts	Sport	2015

A long route on slopey small holds.

The Accent Extension project (17)	P	P	19m	8 bolts	Sport	2016

Continue past the anchor station on The Accent and get ready to jump! The extension ends at two bolts.

18 Spread Eagle	5b	★★★	18m	trad	Sport	2016

The only trad route in Ein Yabrud. It features fun stemming and some sketchy gear placements up the obvious corner crack.

19 Up and Over	6c	★	18m	6 bolts	Sport	2015

Climb the face to the right of the corner.

20 Masar Ibrahim (Abraham's Path)	6c	★★★	17m	6 bolts	Sport	2016

The striking traverse with varied movement! Shares the first two bolts with Up and Over then traverses right in the horizontal crack.

21 Slap the Himar	6c	★	16m	5 bolts	Sport	2016

Technical overhang leads to technical slab. Fun!

22 The First Cut is the Deepest	6a	★★	16m	6 bolts	Sport	2016

Starts around the corner to the right of Slap the Himar. Named for a particularly painful start hold and a beautiful Sheryl Crow song.

Markus Maier on "Masar Ibrahim," 6c (page 55)
Photo by Will Harris

03 . EIN QINIYA ★★★★★

03 EIN QINIYA

Routes	36
Length	12-25m
Rock	Limestone
Political Area	B
Coordinates	31.9373737, 35.1598627

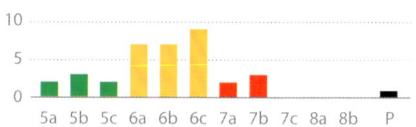

OVERVIEW

Ein Qiniya features beautiful cliffs, which are rarely visited unless by climbers or local Bedouin. Some of the local Bedouin are dedicated climbers with their own gear. The authors of this guidebook started bolting routes in Ein Qiniya in the fall of 2014. However, there was some limited climbing activity in the area before route development began, and the Bedouin have been climbing on these rocks for ages! On any given weekend and some afternoons, you can expect to find Palestinian and foreign climbers enjoying the cliffs.

SEASON

The Ein Qiniya cliffs face southeast and are perfect for climbing all year round. The cliff gets shade from 14:00 to 20:00 in the summer, which makes the location great for afternoon climbing.

Throughout the year, the birds of Ein Qiniya will nest up high in the rocks near some of the routes. If you see baby birds and nests when climbing, please cease climbing and avoid those sectors. Wait a couple weeks until the birds have grown and left the nest. The kestrels have been known to nest high above the Honey Sector. If you do climb during these nesting periods, you may face the wrath of the mother kestrel!

GEAR

Most routes are bolted sport climbs equipped with an anchor station with rappelling ring. Some of the routes can be climbed trad and also end at bolted anchor stations. Most routes will need between 5 and 10 quickdraws. A standard 60 meter rope is the best option.

Crag developers on the approach
Photo by Tim Bruns

Saleh Abu Rakiya on "The Cheesegrater (aka Käsereibe)," 6c (page 68)
Photo by Tim Bruns

EIN QINIYA

DIRECTIONS

Directions (car): From Al-Manara circle in Ramallah, drive west, downhill on the main Rukab Street. Follow the road all the way down through the Al-Tireh neighbourhood and past the last traffic circle. Continue straight down the hill through a number of switchbacks. Turn left on road 463 towards Ein Qiniya village at the bottom of the valley. Follow 463 to the village of Ein Qiniya. Drive through the village and take a right at the intersection near the mosque. Immediately take the right (higher) road down towards the "Zeituna" spring. Nearing the spring, the road will turn from asphalt to dirt. Once you arrive at the spring, take a left (crossing over the spring) and head uphill. Take another left at the intersection and head up the steep dirt road, following as it winds sharply to the right at the top of the hill. Park near the houses at the top of the hill. Hike north up the hill to gain the high ground above the roads and houses. Then head right to the cliffs above the olive groves. The cliffs face southeast directly across the valley from the Reehan hospital (see page 14 Health & Emergency). The trail from the parking area is marked by rock cairns, but some may have fallen down due to weather and goats. Do your best to stay on the trail that looks the most used. If you are worried about your car making it up the hill, just park at the bottom by the spring next to the stone wall.

Directions (public transport): Reaching the cliffs in Ein Qiniya by public transportation is cheap and fun! The service station to Ein Qiniya is located in the parking lot next to the Canadian Embassy (just a 5 minute walk from Al-Manara circle). There are two services that run shuttles to and from the village on weekdays during daylight hours. The weekend connections are far less frequent and almost nonexistent on Fridays. The ride to Ein Qiniya village takes roughly 15 minutes. Once you reach the village, ask the driver to take you further down the valley to the "Zeituna" spring. The trip costs 10 NIS per person to the Zeituna spring (this can be negotiated closer to 5 NIS if you have "wasta" which is a commonly used term to describe connections to influential people). From there, follow the directions above to reach the cliff. Majdi is the main service driver; he will teach you some Arabic poetry if you'd like!

EIN QINIYA

ETIQUETTE
Climbers have formed a good relationship with the local Ein Qiniya municipality and gained permission and support for climbing activity at the cliffs. It is vital that visitors perpetuate the good relationship with the local community by being respectful and culturally sensitive. The local Bedouin boys love to climb so invite them to join! They would be happy to redpoint your 6c project in sandals.

Local Bedouin climbers (Arabic only):
Sagur: +972 59 966 9134
Tawfiq: +972 59 878 3708

CRAG DEVELOPERS
Tim Bruns, Will Harris, Dario Franchetti, Kim Van Der Putten, Andrea Bernardi, Benjamin Korff, Camille Dupouy, Selim Schweitzer, Markus Maier, David Jakob, and Matt Harms.

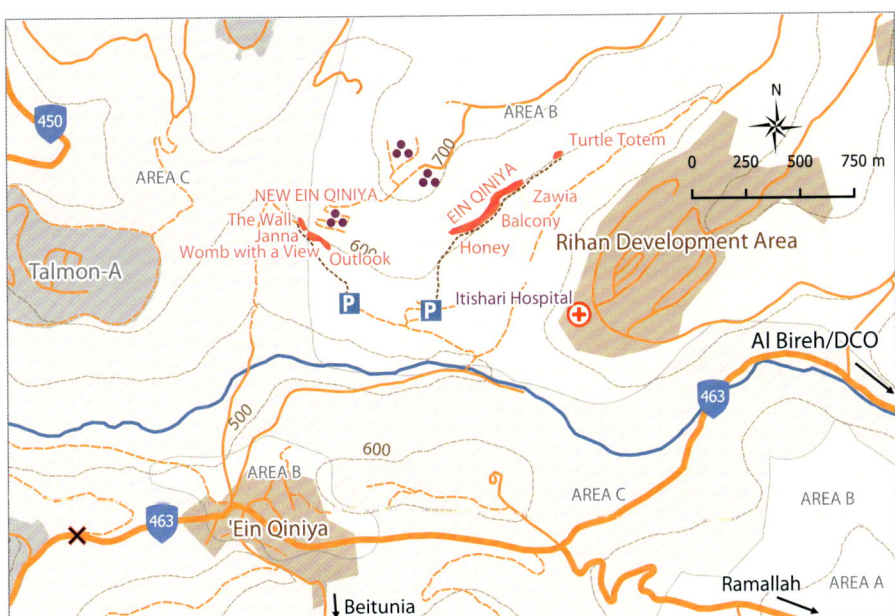

BOULDERING IN EIN QINIYA
In addition to the sport climbing cliffs, the Ein Qiniya valley hosts a number of boulders, of which only a few have been climbed and established. If you are a boulderer, there are new problems to be discovered and climbed! Some boulders are located on the terraces directly below the Honey Sector. For more potential, try hiking along the valley to the west where other boulders have been spotted but not properly established. The problems get less traffic than the sport routes so climbers should bring cleaning equipment and exercise caution. If you establish new boulders, let us know about them!

EIN QINIYA | HONEY SECTOR

 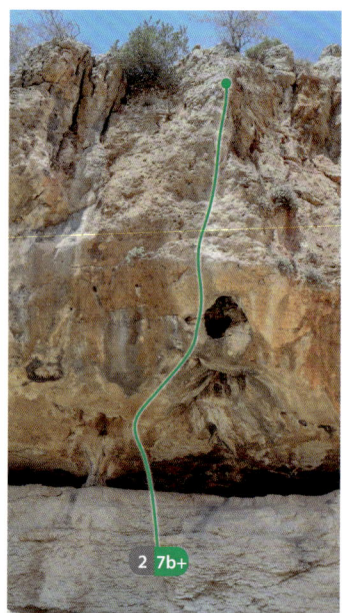

HONEY SECTOR

ROUTE	GRADE	RATING	METERS	BOLTS	STYLE	DEVELOPED
1 Last Call	7b+	★★	18m	6 bolts	Sport	2018

Tough beginning, rewarding end. To clean the route, either top-rope it or rappel from the third bolt where you should find a quicklink (maillon).

2 Trou de Cul	7b+	★★	17m	5 bolts	Sport	2015

Wade your way through the roof full of pigeon droppings... The rope drag makes dynamic belaying impossible in the vertical sections (and has resulted in a broken ankle). Extend the 4th quickdraw to make sure you have a safe fall.

Urwah Askar on "Angry Birds," 6a+ (page 65)
Photo by Ray Wood

EIN QINIYA | HONEY SECTOR

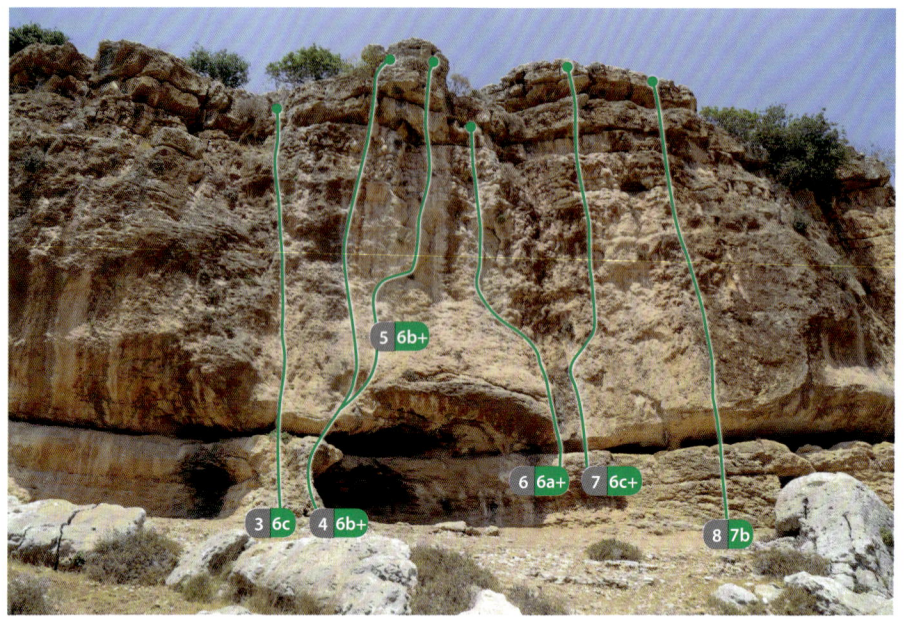

HONEY SECTOR

ROUTE	GRADE	RATING	METERS	BOLTS	STYLE	DEVELOPED
3 Diplomatic Status	6c	★★★	19m	7 bolts	Sport	2015
Starts left of the cave and follows the natural line.						
4 Swingman	6b+	★★★	25m	7 bolts	Sport	2015
Hang on for the first move then follow the bolts up the face for varied movement and fun climbing. Harder for short climbers.						
5 Hangman	6b+		26m	7 bolts	Sport	2015
Most exposed route in Ein Qiniya with a daring double overhang finish. Beware of flakey rock in the top section!						
6 Yom Asel	6a+	★★	20m	7 bolts	Sport	2015
Climb the corner and traverse left over the cave. Enjoy the first and one of the and best climbs in Ein Qiniya!						
7 The Flying Dutchman	6c+	★★★	25m	9 bolts	Sport	2015
Directly to the right of Yom Asel, the Flying Dutchman follows small holds up the face.						
8 Valhalla	7b	★★	25m	4 bolts	Sport	2016
The first move favors tall people.						

Tawfiq Najada on
"The Flying Dutchman," 6c+ (page 62)
Photo by Adam Rouhana

EIN QINIYA | HONEY SECTOR

HONEY SECTOR

ROUTE	GRADE	RATING	METERS	BOLTS	STYLE	DEVELOPED
9 Kareem Abdul Jabar	6a	★	14m	5 bolts	Sport	2015
The route gets its name for the first, very reachy move. Unfair for short people, and don't feel bad to use a cheater rock.						
10 Shawarma Blues	5c+	★★	14m	5 bolts	Sport	2015
Ends at the same anchor as Kareem Abdul Jabar.						
11 Nutcracked	5b	★	16m	0 bolts	trad	2014
The only trad route in Ein Qiniya, this fun 5b follows the natural crack. When the crack ends, traverse right to reach anchor above the overhang.						
12 Pink Scarf	6b+	★★	16m	6 bolts	Sport	2014
Delicate and sustained climbing.						

BALCONY SECTOR | EIN QINIYA

BALCONY SECTOR

ROUTE	GRADE	RATING	METERS	BOLTS	STYLE	DEVELOPED
13 Maramia	5a	★★	12m	4 bolts	Sport	2015

A great slab climb for first-time climbers or leaders. We recommend a quickdraw in the second bolt to protect the swing if you are setting up a top-rope.

14 Fayrooz Al Halwa	6b	★	12 m	4 bolts	Sport	2015

Technical climbing that starts at the crack and traverses left.

15 Maikel's Balls	6c	★	14m	4 bolts	Sport	2018

Named after a Dutch ice climber whose bolts were donated to us. Tiny crimps and technical moves.

16 Corn Flake	6c	★★	14m	5 bolts	Sport	2015

The difficult moves on the suspect flake lead to a crack that is not as good as it looks...

17 Angry Birds	6a+	★★★	15m	5 bolts	Sport	2015

Beautiful gym-style climbing makes this route an instant classic.

18 Will Climb For Donor Money	6b	★	15m	5 bolts	Sport	2015

Dynamic, overhanging moves make this a unique climb in Ein Qiniya. Don't blow the third clip or you may hit the ledge! Loose rock in the lower section.

EIN QINIYA | BALCONY SECTOR

BALCONY SECTOR

ROUTE	GRADE	RATING	METERS	BOLTS	STYLE	DEVELOPED
19 Al-Osh	5b	★★	13m	4 bolts	Sport	2015
A great climb for beginners with 3-dimensional climbing and lots of stemming! We wish it were four times the length.							
20 Al Shatr Bidhak Fil Akhir	6a+	★★	14m	4 bolts	Sport	2016
The translation means: The one who laughs last laughs the best. Not as easy as it looks.							
21 Take Me to Deutschland	7a+	★★	13m	4 bolts	Sport	2015
Bouldery, dynamic moves.							
22 Butt vs. Gravity	6c+	★★	13m	5 bolts	Sport	2016
Short but fun. Desperate moves in an unforgiving overhang.							

ZAWIA SECTOR | EIN QINIYA

ZAWIA SECTOR LEFT

ROUTE	GRADE	RATING	METERS	BOLTS	STYLE	DEVELOPED
23 Sharq Face	6c	★	12m	4 bolts	Sport	2016
Climb up to the ledge and start the climb on the left face. Small crimps on great rock.						
24 Al-Zawia	6a	★	13m	4 bolts	Sport	2015
Gain the ledge and walk to the dihedral to start the climb. Follow the natural features in the corner.						
25 Bab	6b	★	13m	4 bolts	Sport	2015
Start this climb on the ledge to the right of Al-Zawia. One move in the middle gives it the name ("Door" in English) and grade!						

EIN QINIYA | ZAWIA SECTOR

ZAWIA SECTOR RIGHT

ROUTE	GRADE	RATING	METERS	BOLTS	STYLE	DEVELOPED
26 Bil Tawfiq (Good Luck)	6c	★	14m	5 bolts	Sport	2017

Clipping the third bolt is dodgy. Good luck with that. We advise to stick-clip the third bolt.

27 Sagur	5b	★	14m	3 bolts	Sport	2015

An awkward, sketchy lead but the interesting movements are good practice for beginners.

28 More Atar Please	6b+	★	14m	4 bolts	Sport	2015

Follow the bolt line on the left side of the corner and pull a small roof!

29 Crazy Dance	6b	★★	14m	5 bolts	Sport	2015

Start to the right and follow sharp holds up to the same anchor as More Atar Please.

30 Jug-or-Not	5a	★★★	14m	4 bolts	Sport	2015

Start to the right of Crazy Dance and follow jugs up large features.

31 The Cheesegrater (aka Käsereibe)	6c	★	14m	4 bolts	Sport or trad	2015

A route for the masochistic. It gets its name for the heinously sharp holds and crack. It's not over when you pull the roof. The route has also been climbed with natural gear in true British fashion by David Jakob.

TURTLE TOTEM | EIN QINIYA

TURTLE TOTEM LEFT To reach this sector, keep walking past the Zawia sector. After about 200 meters you will see the turtle shaped crag.

ROUTE	GRADE	RATING	METERS	BOLTS	STYLE	DEVELOPED
32 Blood Donor Shares the same anchor with Organ Donor (33).	5c	★	13m	4 bolts	Sport	2017
33 Organ Donor Adventurous start.	6a	★	13m	5 bolts	Sport	2017
34 Al Hakim (Nathan der Weise) Powerful overhang. Pay attention to not let your rope go over the sharp water grooves when lowering down.	7a	★★	15m	5 bolts	Sport	2017

EIN QINIYA | TURTLE TOTEM

TURTLE TOTEM RIGHT

ROUTE	GRADE	RATING	METERS	BOLTS	STYLE	DEVELOPED
35 Rambazamba A great powerful line! Sharp but totally worth it.	6c+	★★★	14m	4 bolts	Sport	2017
36 No Contact Policy Merciless. Sharp rock and bouldery moves.	P	★	14m	5 bolts	Sport	2017

Urwah Askar on "Yom Asel," 6a+ (page 62)
Photo by Ray Wood

03 . NEW EIN QINIYA ★★★★☆

04 NEW EIN QINIYA (UNDER THE RUINS)

Routes	21
Length	14-22m
Rock	Limestone
Political Area	B
Coordinates	31.936449, 35.152061

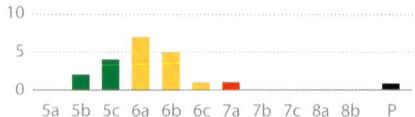

OVERVIEW
Under the Ruins is one of the newer climbing areas in Palestine. Development started in April 2017, and the area has potential for up to 25 routes. The routes here are a bit shorter than in the other climbing areas, but in turn they offer great movements, especially at "The Wall" sector.

SEASON
The cliffs are south-facing, which makes Under the Ruins extremely hot in the summer. The best seasons are definitely winter, spring, and fall. The proximity to Ramallah (15-minute drive) makes it a popular after-work climbing area. From 17:00 until sunset (20:00 in the summer) you can have decent temperatures in the late spring and early autumn.

GEAR
Under the Ruins is a very new climbing area and some of the routes might still have loose rock. Therefore the belayer should definitely wear a helmet. You will need 8 quickdraws and a standard 60 meter rope. Some of the routes can be climbed trad.

CONFLICT
The crag is surrounded by beautiful nature and you will have a splendid view; however, we recommend not camping there, as its proximity to Dolev and Talmon settlements make it problematic at night. A watchtower overlooks the valley, and if you camp there with headlights on or a campfire, this will most likely attract the attention of the soldiers. Do not hike onto the nearby hills or to the cliffs left (west) of New Ein Qiniya. They are close to one of the settlements and some climbers have witnessed local kids being shot at by settlers while collecting herbs.

Sarah Theresa on "The Pearl," 6b (page 79)
Photo by Markus Maier

NEW EIN QINIYA

DIRECTIONS
Same access as to Ein Qiniya, once you are driving up the dirt road after having crossed the small stream go straight where the road makes sharp turn to the right, after 200 meters you will reach the parking spot, the road ends dead. From there scramble up (always in the direction of the buildings) until you reach the Outlook Sector.

CRAG DEVELOPERS
A number of people have contributed to the development of Under the Ruins as a climbing site. The first developers were Markus Maier, Tobias Mohn, Tim Bruns, Inas Radaydeh, Majdal Sobeh, Anas Askar, Gabriel Sawant, and Bastian Schilling.

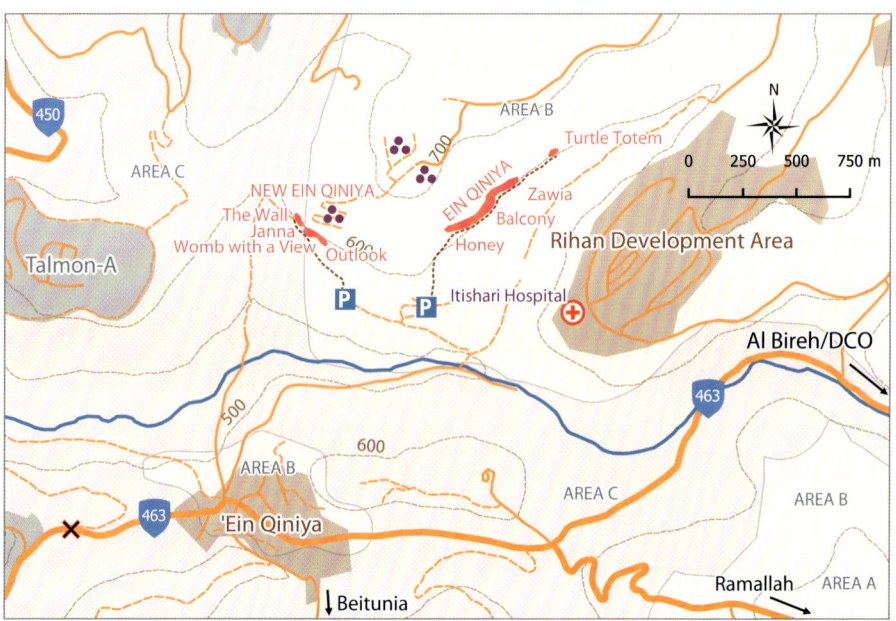

OUTLOOK SECTOR | NEW EIN QINIYA

OUTLOOK SECTOR This is the first sector when you approach the crag from the parking.

ROUTE	GRADE	RATING	METERS	BOLTS	STYLE	DEVELOPED
1 Athan	5c	★	11m	5 bolts	Sport	2018

Nice short route with a harder start.
The debate of whether or not it is ok to bolt during Athan (the call to prayer) is still not settled.

2 Um	5b	★★	13m	5 bolts	Sport	2017

The direct beginning is a bit more difficult. Alternatively start further right and crawl through the crack. Good warm up and beginners' route.

3 Lump	6b	★	12m	4 bolts	Sport	2017

Once you reach the ledge at the end, traverse over to the anchor of Um.

NEW EIN QINIYA | WOMB WITH A VIEW

WOMB WITH A VIEW

ROUTE	GRADE	RATING	METERS	BOLTS	STYLE	DEVELOPED
4 Khudra wa Fawaqeh Make good use of that chimney!	6a	★★★	12m	4 bolts	Sport	2018
5 Fools Rush In Tricky, don't rush in.	6a	★★	13m	5 bolts	Sport	2017
6 Cry Me A Wadi Stay out of the crack. It does not make it easier and there is nice face climbing to the right.	5c	★	13m	4 bolts	Sport	2017
7 Marcinalisation In the beginning traverse a bit left into the route. At the fourth bolt go left and mantle onto the plateau.	5b+	★	13m	5 bolts	Sport	2017

JANNA SECTOR | NEW EIN QINIYA

JANNA (HEAVEN) SECTOR RIGHT

ROUTE	GRADE	RATING	METERS	BOLTS	STYLE	DEVELOPED
8 Lunatics	5c+	★★★	15m	4 bolts	Sport	2017

Great climb. Follow the line through the cracks. Gets harder at the end.

9 A Plumber's Smile	6a+	★	17m	6 bolts	Sport	2017

Tough start, tough end, like many routes at this crag.

10 Rhino	6b	★★	17m	7 bolts	Sport	2017

Stand up on the rhino's horn.

11 The Next Chapter	6a+	★	19m	7 bolts	Sport	2017

Shares first bolt and the anchor station with Steve (12).

12 Steve	6a	★	19m	7 bolts	Sport	2017

Yeah, why not name a route after a random British guy whose name wasn't even Steve?

NEW EIN QINIYA | JANNA SECTOR | THE WALL

JANNA SECTOR LEFT SIDE   THE WALL RIGHT SIDE

ROUTE	GRADE	RATING	METERS	BOLTS	STYLE	DEVELOPED
13 Baba's Route	6a+	★	13m	5 bolts	Sport	2018

Technical climb. The route shares 3 bolts with Demolition Order. If you climb left of the bolts it is 5c, if you climb right of the bolts it is 6a+.

14 Demolition Order	5c	★	13m	4 bolts	Sport	2018

Shares 3 bolts with Baba's Route.

THE WALL
On this wall all routes are excellent. After an adventurous start you have perfect lines on superb rock ahead of you.

15 Tasrih	6b	★★★	14m	5 bolts	Sport	2018

Sustained. Shares an anchor with West Bank Only.

16 West Bank Only	6b+	★★★	14m	4 bolts	Sport	2017

Getting past the overhang is not easy, and it is not over after that...

17 Zift Maqli (boiled asphalt)	6b+	★★★	14m	5 bolts	Sport	2017

One of the nicest routes in the country. Great fun. Direct start is really tough, alternatively come in from the right side, but pay attention to loose rock.

THE WALL | NEW EIN QINIYA

THE WALL LEFT SIDE

ROUTE	GRADE	RATING	METERS	BOLTS	STYLE	DEVELOPED
18 High Expectations	7a+	★★	15m	5 bolts	Sport	2017
Pre-clip strongly recommended. Hard moves on great rock.						
19 Project (not fully bolted)	P		15m	0 bolts	Sport	2018
Really tough moves from the overhang to the face.						
20 Zineb's Curse	6c+	★★	15m	5 bolts	Sport	2017
Daring moves.						
21 The Pearl	6b	★★★	14m	6 bolts	Sport	2017
The nicest route at the crag. An absolute must. Adventurous start, tough period after finish.						

05 . AL BIREH ★★★★★

05 AL BIREH MAKTABNA (OUR OFFICE)

Routes	16 (potential for 40)
Length	14m
Rock	Limestone
Political Area	C
Coordinates	31.909685, 35.233887

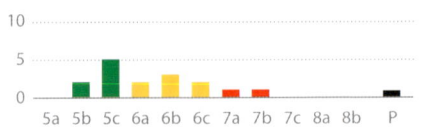

OVERVIEW
Although the authors have known about the Al-Bireh cliff for a while, climbing development began only recently (fall 2018). Its location in a calm valley surrounded by some of the most conflict-prone areas of the West Bank made us reluctant to explore the site for a long time. However, when we did, we immediately regretted not having started to climb there earlier. Its proximity to Ramallah makes for a great afternoon climbing spot. Additionally, all but two routes are on a north-facing cliff, which is important in Palestine during the months of burning summer heat. There is still potential for some medium and harder routes.

SAFETY PRECAUTIONS:
The rock is slightly softer than in the other areas, so watch out and wear a helmet. Due to the proximity to the notorious DCO checkpoint, the settlement of Psagot, and Mulberry Spring Road (which is predominantly used by settlers) we recommend keeping a low profile. Do not hike up onto the nearby hills, and if you encounter Palestinians make it clear where you are from, as there are often protesters on the other (northern) side of the hill. Depending on your group, you could be mistaken for settlers, so communicate proactively with anyone around and explain that you are here for climbing. Do not park on Mulberry Spring Road, but follow the approach described below! The vehicle will most likely be inspected by the military.

AL BIREH

DIRECTIONS

By car: To reach the cliff, you will have to drive through the labyrinth of the Al Bireh industrial area. Thus, we recommend you use the GPS location to reach the parking space. At some point you will have to exit the street onto a dirt road—the GPS coordinates for that point are as follows 31.910688, 35.22438—park your car at that bend.

By public transport: There is no public transport to this area. Take a taxi to the Al Bireh Stadium and walk towards the GPS parking location. From the parking area, follow a small path for 10 minutes into the valley (direction east). Keep on the right side of the wadi. After a kilometer or so you will eventually reach the cliff which will appear on your right.

Ewa on "Overhead Costs," 6a+ (page 82)
Photo by Matthias Wurtenberger

AL BIREH | SOUTHERN CLIFF

RIGHT SIDE

SOUTHERN CLIFF RIGHT

ROUTE	GRADE	RATING	METERS	BOLTS	STYLE	Developed
1. Too Hard for Today Much harder than it looks.	7a+	★	10m	3 bolts	Sport	2018
2. Hidden Agenda The name should give you a clue about the route...	6b+	★★	12m	4 bolts	Sport	2018
3. Overhead Costs Some routes just have it all, big jugs, campus moves, overhang and even some crack climbing.	6a+	★★★	13m	4 bolts	Sport	2018
4. Bloody Fingers Slabby crux after a piercy start.	6b+	★	12m	3 bolts	Sport	2018

SOUTHERN CLIFF | AL BIREH

SOUTHERN CLIFF MIDDLE

ROUTE	GRADE	RATING	METERS	BOLTS	STYLE	DEVELOPED
5. Saufen Tough start up the overhang.	6c	★★	12m	4 bolts	Sport	2018
6. Wild Boar Shares the first two bolts with Mutaarij, then traverses to the right. Pumpy and great holds. Use a sling when cleaning the traverse to avoid swinging!	6a+	★★★	15m	7 Bolts		2019
7. Mutaarij Plenty of choices while the routes crawls up like a snake.	5b		12m	4 bolts	Sport	2018

AL BIREH | SOUTHERN CLIFF

SOUTHERN CLIFF MIDDLE

ROUTE	GRADE	RATING	METERS	BOLTS	STYLE	DEVELOPED
8. Ahjee!	5c+		10m	3 bolts	Sport	2019

Straight up—the first moves are much harder for shorter people.

9. Half Moon	5c+		10m	4 bolts	Sport	2019

Same start as "Ahjee!", go left around the big hole as you ascend.

10. Pocket Pick	6b		11m	3 bolts	Sport	2019

Jam your fingers in the pockets and up you go. Same anchor as Hunch Back (11).

11. Hunch Back	5c		10m	3 bolts	Sport	2018

East-facing tower climb. Tough first move, then easy climb.

NORTHERN CLIFF | AL BIREH

NORTHERN CLIFF

Development on the northern side of the valley has just begun (April 2019), with potential for more than 16 routes. Even by Palestine standards, the limestone here is incredibly sharp and spikey. The variety of potential styles is also great: from slab, to overhang to crack climbing. Soon there will be plenty of additional routes welcoming the curious climber.

ROUTE	GRADE	RATING	METERS	BOLTS	STYLE	DEVELOPED
12 Maniak Project Steep overhang, little pockets	7b		12m	4 bolts	Sport	2019
13 **a. No Karsh Needed** Climb up the overhang face and enjoy the beauty of moves required here.	6c	★★★	11m	3 bolts	Sport	2019
b. Al Kasul Alternatively, and more easy-going—ignore the face and go up the crack on the right, traversing left once you are on the ledge.	5c					
14 Buzbutish Climb up with the crack on your left.	5b		14m	5 bolts	Sport	2019
15 Handover Straight up, unlike some handovers at work. Shares anchor with Buzbutish (14).	5c		14m	5 bolts	Sport	2019
16 Harami Start at the left of the cave using the crack above it and go up diagonally to the left. Shares anchor with Buzbutish (14).	5b		14m	5 bolts	Sport	2019

06 . EIN FARA ★★★★★

06 EIN FARA

Routes	>130
Length	15-35m
Rock	Limestone
Political Area	C
Coordinates	31.8349 N, 35.2983 E

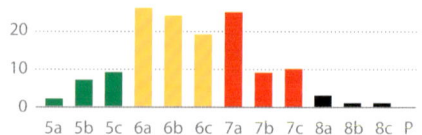

OVERVIEW

Ein Fara is considered one of the best sport climbing sites in the Middle East, both for the quality and the quantity of the climbing and for the spectacular location. Ein Fara, know as "Ein Prat" by Israelis, was first developed as a climbing site in the 1980s when some Israeli climbers opened the first mixed (trad/sport) routes. In the 1990s and 2000s sport climbing development increased and many new, beautiful routes were equipped. Today, the potential for expansion of the site is still huge, both for rope climbing and bouldering. Unfortunately, the Israel Nature and Parks Authority has banned the development of any additional climbing outside the signposted areas. A black '✖' will appear next to individual routes that were closed at the time of publishing this book

All in all, there are more than 130 routes in Ein Fara equally distributed over two areas: the Northern Cliff and the Southern Cliff. Unfortunately, a large number of existing climbs have been closed by the Israel Nature and Parks Authority. In the past, other developed sectors have even had the bolts chopped! If you are caught climbing in any of the closed sectors, expect to pay a fine of 300 NIS or more.

Hiking trail up the valley

EIN FARA

SEASON
Ein Fara is exposed to the north, south, and west, and it is possible to climb all through the year (although in summer, particularly in July and August, it can be hot even in the shade). The Northern Wall is mainly south-exposed: very pleasant on winter days, but in summer only climbable in the morning before it is hit by the sun. The Southern Wall is north and east exposed with changing patterns of shade and sun during the day. Most of the harder routes get shade in the afternoon, while the beginners sectors are shady in the morning.

GEAR
Most routes are bolted sport climbs and are equipped with an anchor station and rappel ring. Most of the trad routes also end at bolted anchor stations (except those specified in the routes descriptions). Most routes will need between 8 and 12 quickdraws. A standard 70 meter rope is the best option. A small number of double pitches can be climbed on the Southern Wall.

Photo by Miranda Oakley

ACCESS
Ein Fara is the westernmost, upstream part of Wadi Qelt; a beautiful and, in parts, lush valley connecting the central West Bank with the Jordan Valley. It was once the main source of water and grazing land for the Bedouin and Palestinian villagers living east of Jerusalem.

After 1967 and the occupation of the West Bank by the State of Israel, the "designation of use" of the land was changed and Ein Fara is now an "Israeli Nature Reserve" dominated by the Israeli settlement of Almon/Anatot. Access to natural resources and the use of land is now severely limited for Palestinians in these areas.

Access to the climbing area is a sensitive issue. There are three ways to enter the reserve to climb, and, like many things in the West Bank, how you enter depends on your ID. Once you reach the gate of the Anatot settlement, access to West Bank Palestinians and green-plated Palestinian cars is forbidden. Foreigners, Israelis, and Palestinians with Jerusalem IDs are allowed to enter the settlement in yellow-plated Israeli cars. Palestinians

EIN FARA

with West Bank IDs, therefore, have two options: drive around the settlement on an unmarked dirt road (as described below) or park outside the gates of the Anatot settlement and hike roughly 45 minutes to the climbing area. Many internationals and Palestinians opt for the longer hike into the valley to avoid paying the 29 NIS fee charged by the Israel Nature and Parks Authority and to refrain from financially supporting the Israeli occupation of Palestinian land. The three ways to enter the reserve are described below:

Walking Option (note: if you walk, you are only allowed to climb at the Southern Wall without paying the nature park entrance fee): From the car park situated just outside the yellow gate of Anatot settlement, everybody is allowed to walk down on a hiking trail towards Ein Fara; no entrance fee is required. Park on the right side of the road just before the yellow gate. Cross the road and walk along the settlement fence. Most likely, the guards at the settlement will be watching you, but you are not breaking any law. After a few minutes, you will reach a trail with green and white markers that descends the valley for about 25 minutes. At the end of a flat walking section (200-300 meters), leave the marked path and walk down to the left towards the visible cliff at the next corner of the valley (total time to reach the Southern Wall: 30-45 minutes). Climbing at the Southern Wall does not require payment of the entry fee. If you keep walking down to the Northern Wall, you are supposed to pay the entry fee to the Israel Nature and Parks Authority.

There is a ranger station by the parking lot in the bottom of the valley (past the climbing areas), where you may be allowed to pay although the official place to pay is at the vehicular entrance to the reserve (described below).

Driving Option (for West Bank Palestinians/Palestinian vehicles): From Hizma keep driving towards Jericho. Pass the Anata junction (do not turn to the left towards Anatot settlement/Ein Prat), keep driving for 300-400 meters and turn to the left at the next dirt road (passable without 4x4 unless it's very wet). Follow the dirt road, and at the first junction with another dirt road take a left and keep driving until the entrance of the nature reserve (10 minutes). At the entrance of the nature reserve you will still need to pay the entrance fee! After paying, drive down into the valley and park at the last parking area. From there you can hike to and climb at the Northern or Southern Wall.

Driving Option (for foreigners, Israelis, Jerusalemites/ Israeli vehicles): Yellow plated cars (registered in Israel) are allowed to drive through the Anatot settlement to reach the entrance of the "Ein Prat" nature reserve. After passing through the settlement, pay the fee at the entrance to the reserve and continue down into the valley.

The park closes at 15:00 in winter and 16:00 in summer (earlier on Saturdays). If you drive into the reserve, you have to leave before closing time. If you walk down you can stay climbing until after the reserve closes.

EIN FARA

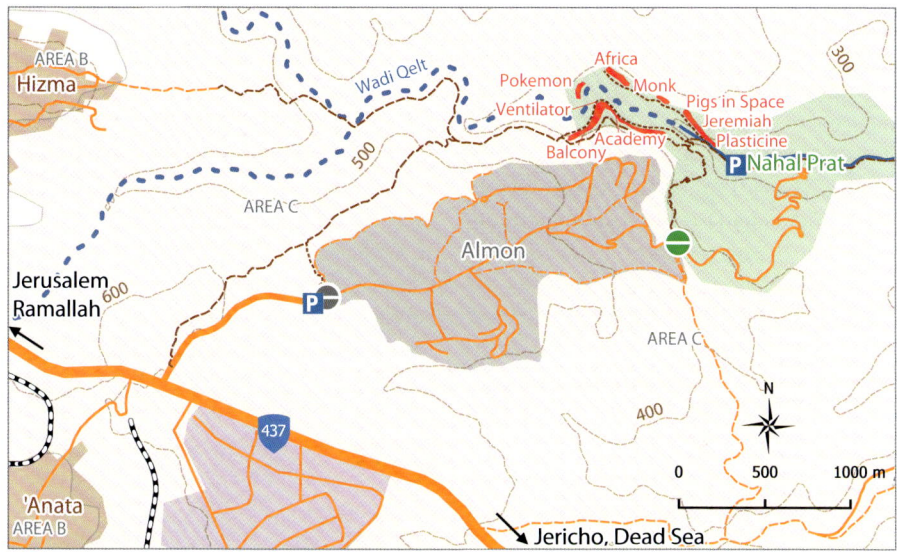

DIRECTIONS

From Jerusalem (15 min. by car): Leave the city through the Hizma (Pisgat Ze'ev) checkpoint and take a right at the first roundabout towards Jericho. After about 1 km, you will reach a junction with a brown signpost on your left indicating the way to Ein Fara (it is refered to as "Ein Prat" on the signpost). Take a left and drive until you reach the entry gate of the Israeli settlement of Almon/Anatot.

From Ramallah (20 min. by car): Drive south past Qalandia checkpoint and continue past the Jaba checkpoint until you reach the junction (Jaba circle). Take a sharp right at the circle towards Hizma and Jerusalem. When you reach the next roundabout at the Hizma checkpoint, continue south (left) towards Jericho. From here, follow the directions given when coming from Jerusalem (above).

*If you are in a green-plated Palestinian car or you are with Palestinians from the West Bank (green IDs), you are **NOT** allowed to enter the Almon (Anatot) settlement.*

EIN FARA

OTHER ACTIVITIES

Beside rock climbing, Ein Fara offers amazing possibilities to enjoy the Palestinian environment, history, and geography:

Ein Fara is a starting point of the second section of the Wadi Qelt hike (the entire walk runs from Hizma to Jericho, taking 8-11 hours. Elevation change: 650 ascent; 1500 descent). The route is the ancient path between Jerusalem and the Jordan valley. On the way, you will pass monasteries, Roman water channels that are still functioning, Bedouin herder communities grazing their animals, and interesting fauna (gazelles, ibex, hyracks, foxes, eagles, snakes, fish, and birds) and flora (orchid, iris, peony, oak and olive trees, pistachios, eucalyptus... and others). Highly recommended is the beautiful walk to Ein Fawwar (3-4 hours) and Jericho (third section: 4-6 hours). For further information, we suggest the hiking guidebook "Walking in Palestine", written by Stefan Szepesi, published by Interlink Walking Guides (available at the Educational Book Shop in Jerusalem and at Wadi Climbing Gym in Ramallah).

Pools: Ein Fara is a spring and has several natural pools where it's possible to swim and relax in the fresh water. Bring swimming clothes on hot days!

Note: Swimming in pools is only permitted by the Israeli Nature Reserve Authority if you have paid the entrance fee.

Ein Fara also offers deep water bouldering in its pools further down the valley
Photo by unknown

EIN FARA

CRAG DEVELOPERS
A number of people have contributed to the development of Ein Fara. Among them are: Andrea Anati, Gili Tenne, Leron Axelrod, Nir P., Yoav Nir, Arik Lerner, Yotam Orchan, Tal Niv, Itay Levine, Dima Stragnov, Nimrod Nachmias, Omer Shavit, Yonatav Barlev, Moti Elkalai, and Ofer Blutrich.

NORTHERN WALL
The Northern Wall is comprised of a number of sectors that start close to the Nature Reserve parking lot and ends high up the wadi across from the Ventilator Sector of the Southern Wall. Unfortunately, many routes have been temporarily closed by the Israel Nature and Parks Authority. The sectors are mainly exposed to the south, so there will be shade in the morning. On sunny winter days you can climb here in a t-shirt. During the summer, bring a swimsuit to enjoy the pools of the fresh water spring.

To climb (and swim) here, payment of the reserve's entrance fee is required (see 'Access' section above). Please also note that, unfortunately, it is not allowed to climb after the closure hours (15:00 in winter and 16:00 in summer). It is possible to move to the Southern Wall (which is located outside the payment area) to climb until sunset, but you need to park your car up the valley, outside the Israeli Settlement (see 'Access' section above).

EIN FARA | PLASTICINE SECTOR

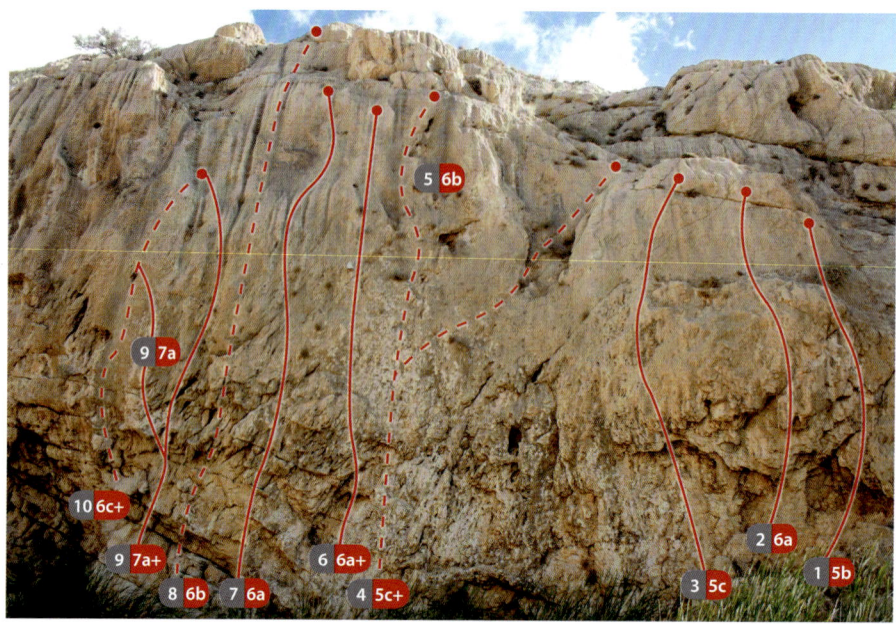

PLASTICINE SECTOR This is the first sector on your right when you come from the Nature Reserve parking lot. It was temporarily closed in 2013 after a small landslide to the east of the sector (visible from the parking lot). Check the situation before climbing here.

ROUTE	GRADE	RATING	METERS	BOLTS	STYLE	DEVELOPED
1 Hands of the Revolution	5b		14m	unknown	Sport	2011
Easy line, slightly traversing left.						
2 Prologue	6a	★★★	16m	16 bolts	Sport	
Starts on the small balcony.						
3 Good New World	5c	★★	18m	6 bolts	Sport	1997
Easy warm up.						
4 Plasticine	5c+	★★★	28m	3 bolts	Mixed	
Classic and well-protected trad line with 3 bolts towards the end and a secure anchor. Bring slings, small and medium cams, nuts, and tricams.						
5 Chocolate Noir	6b	★★	25m	9 bolts	Trad	1997
The climb finishes with beautiful vertical water grooves.						
6 Just One Small Move More?	6a+	★★	25m	9 bolts	Sport	1996
Delicate at the beginning and water grooves on the top.						

EIN FARA

ROUTE	GRADE	RATING	METERS	BOLTS	STYLE	DEVELOPED
7 Children's Game	6b	★★	20m	unknown	Sport	1996

Overhanging start, slabby at the end.

8 Arubota'im	6a	★★★	27m	4 bolts	Mixed	

Mixed trad line. Nuts, slings, and tricams for the overhanging beginning. Bolts are present in the second half of the route. Anchor at the top.

9 Cocaine	7a+	★		unknown	Sport	1996

Finish at the anchor of route 10. If you link it to Children's Game it is a 7a. Overhanging start and final slab.

10 July-August Heat	6c+	★★★	20m	4 bolts	Mixed	1993

Mixed route. Overhanging start and final slab. Four bolts and anchor on the top. Bring slings, tricams and nuts, or small friends.

Shuntaro Suzaki on "Tension," 7a+ (page 94)
Photo by Ryuji Okabe

EIN FARA | JEREMIAH SECTOR

JEREMIAH SECTOR A number of hard, but nice lines and a few easier ones located higher up on the left of the sector. Come early in summer to stay out of the sun. Crossing Red Lines (8c) is currently the hardest established route in the West Bank.

ROUTE	GRADE	RATING	METERS	BOLTS	STYLE	DEVELOPED
11 The Peg	6b+	★★	25m	unknown	Mixed	1993
Mixed trad. Slings for the overhanging beginning, then nuts, tricams, small friends. Two bolts at the crux and anchor on the top.						
12 Tension	7a+	★★★	25m	unknown	Sport	1996
Overhanging start followed by a technical slab.						
13 New Left	7b	★★★	28 m	unknown	Sport	1996
Similar to the previous one, but harder.						
14 Crossing Red Lines	8c	★★	25m	unknown	Sport	2008
Hard, overhanging start and very delicate vertical wall climbing at the end.						
15 Cairo Slammer	7c	★★	15m	unknown	Sport	1998
Tough overhanging start.						
16 Jeremiah	7c+	★★★	15m	unknown	Sport	
Pumpy, overhanging start followed by a slab.						

ROUTE	GRADE	RATING	METERS	BOLTS	STYLE	DEVELOPED
Variation to Jeremiah (16)	7b+		25 m	13 bolts	Sport	2008

Start on the first 3 bolts of Jeremiah (2nd left), then one bolt on Cairo Slammer (left), one intermediate bolt and finish on Crossing Red lines bolts and anchor.

17 Dio Santo	7a	★★	28m	12 bolts	Sport	1998

In the middle section traverse a bit to the right, but don't chicken out to the right too early. Easy for the grade.

18 Ice Tea	6b+	★★	20m	11 bolts	Sport	2006

Small roof at the beginning followed by a more technical section.

19 Lola	6a+	★★	19m	7 bolts	Sport	1998

Start stepping on the boulder, face the technical slab and climb through the crack. Shares the station with Ice Tea (18).

Variation to Lola (19)	6b			10 bolts	Sport	

Before the final crack traverse to the left and end at the station of Short Espresso (20).

20 Short Espresso	6a+	★★	20m	9 bolts	Sport	

Short overhanging start off the boulder, then technical slab. Cruxy.

21 Oldie	6b		20m	unknown	Trad	1995

Big traverse to the right. Old pitons along the way. Ends at the Jeremiah anchor. Slings, nuts, small, friends, tricams.

22 The Garden Crack	5c		20m	unknown	Trad	

Nuts, tricams or small friends, slings. End at the anchor of Short Espresso.

EIN FARA | PIGS IN SPACE SECTOR

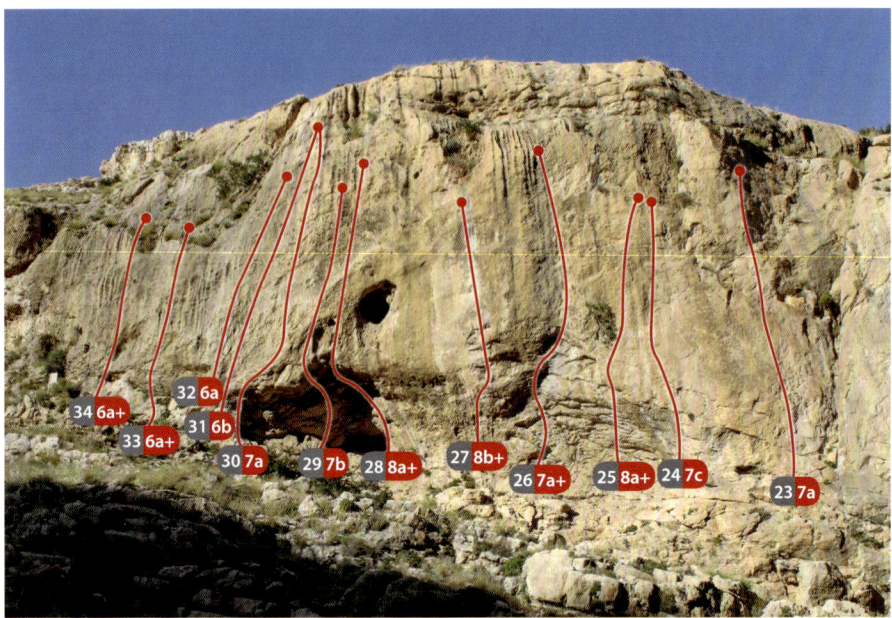

PIGS IN SPACE SECTOR More hard routes, but also a few warm-ups on the far left of the sector. Same exposure as Jeremiah—come early for shade. Please note that route 29 (The Suitcase) is currently closed to climbing.

ROUTE	GRADE	RATING	METERS	BOLTS	STYLE	DEVELOPED
23 Kishkashta	7a	★★	28m	10 bolts	Sport	2007
Start in the crack and then traverse to the right.						
24 Long Espresso	7c	★★	20m	11 bolts	Sport	1996
Engaging and delicate face climb. Caffeine for your fingers.						
25 In Memory of Yoav Nir	8a+	★★	20m	8 bolts	Sport	1998
Strong and technical line. Yoav Nir, maybe the first Israeli climber of some international renown, passed away in 1997 from cancer at the age of 27.						
26 Pigs in Space	7a+	★★★	23m	8 bolts	Sport	1988
Classic! Pumpy, long moves through the overhang.						
27 Russians in Space	8b+	★★★	20 m	unknown	Sport	
Tough overhanging start followed by a technical slab.						
28 Iraqi Celebration	8a+	★★★	18m	8 bolts	Sport	
Tough overhanging start inside the cave followed by a technical slab.						

PIGS IN SPACE SECTOR | EIN FARA

ROUTE	GRADE	RATING	METERS	BOLTS	STYLE	DEVELOPED
29 The Suitcase ✖	7b		21m	11 bolts	Sport	1997

Through the cave to the face. Temporarily closed because of bad rock quality in the cave.

30 Salmonella	7a	★★★	22m	9 bolts	Sport	2006

Start on the left of the cave, then move right after the second bolt.

31 Jigsaw Puzzle	6b	★★★	23m	4 bolts	Mixed	1982

Start on the right of the cave following the crack, placing your own protection. There are 4 bolts coming up at the slab leading up to a bolted station. Take small friends and nuts with you.

32 Hammurabi's Flute	6a	★	20m	7 bolts	Sport	2006

Small roof at the beginning followed by a balance-y slab.

33 Lady S	6a+		17m	6 bolts	Sport	2006

Pumpy. Slightly overhanging beginning on small crimps.

34 Cops and Thieves	6a+		21m	8 bolts	Sport	1998

Delicate and technical beginning followed by easy terrain.

Dario Franchetti on "Dvivon," 7c (page 108)
Photo by unknown

EIN FARA | MONK SECTOR

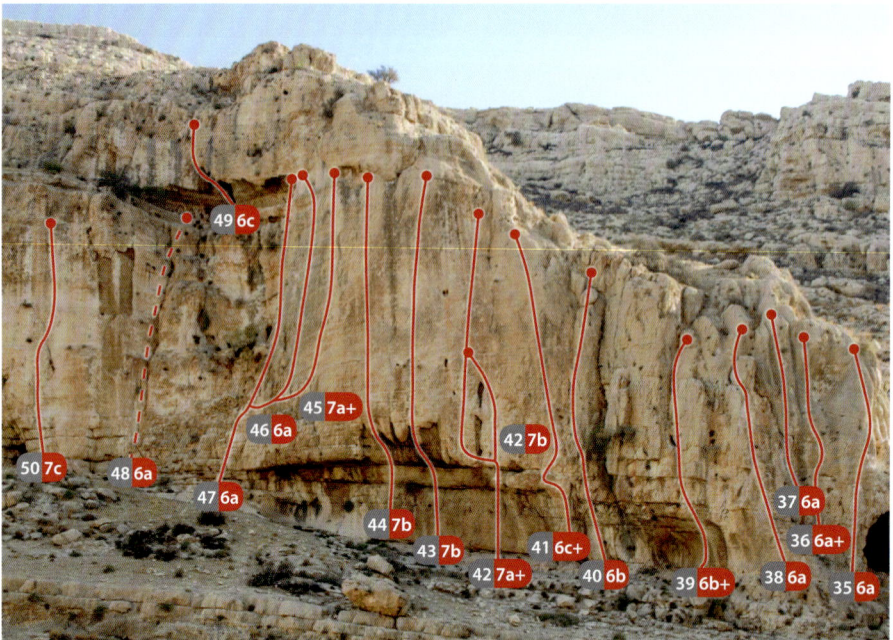

MONK SECTOR You will find the Monk after a 5-minute walk/scramble up the wadi from Pigs in Space. This sector was named after a monk who used to live in a cave situated to the left of of "The Nun" (47). He was kicked out by the Israeli Authorities in 2005.

The Monk sector is usually less busy than the other sectors on the Northern Wall since it is a bit further from the parking lot. At the time of writing of this guidebook only seven routes were open for climbing, but they are well worth the walk. Routes 35-40 and 48-58 have previously been temporary closed by the Israel Nature and Parks Authority. A more recent sign (by the National Park Authority) at the cliff indicates that only the routes left of number 47 (The Nun) are closed. Please check the current status before climbing.

The first four routes below are located on a smaller side wall around the corner from the main face of the Monk.

MONK SECTOR | EIN FARAH

ROUTE	GRADE	RATING	METERS	BOLTS	STYLE	DEVELOPED
35 The Virgin	6a	★★	24m	9 bolts	Sport	2006
The first route on the left of the obvious cave.						
36 The Whore	6a+	★★	27m	9 bolts	Sport	2006
To the left of The Virgin, goes up a little on the right of the grey streak.						
37 Naim ve Tipusi	6a		27m	unknown	Sport	2010
Starts on the left of the central crack.						
38 Crazy Orange	6a		26m	unknown	Sport	2010
The last route on the left of the side-wall.						
39 Lady with Bags	6b+	★★	26m	10 bolts	Sport	2010
Follows the little crack traversing slightly to the left, somewhat overhanging.						
40 "Yakar mi Paz"	6b	★★	28m	12 bolts	Sport	2010
On the left of the big crack in the middle of the main sector. Glue-in bolts.						
41 State of Monk	6c+	★★★	28m	9 bolts	Sport	2007
Physical start on the right of the big sign—long nice route. Runout, but easy after the last bolt.						
42 Unnamed	7a+	★★★	18m	8 bolts	Sport	1997
Overhanging start, chose the left line through the big crack and then go straight up the face.						
Variation to Unnamed (42)	7b		18m	8 bolts	Sport	
Same as number 42, but choose the right and more direct line. Clip accordingly.						
43 PK 32	7b	★★	35m	unknown	Sport	1997
Starts overhanging, ends more vertical.						
44 PK 34	7b	★★	35m	unknown	Sport	1997
Similar to PK32, but steeper at the start.						
45 Unnamed	7a+	★★	>35m (!)	8 bolts	Sport	1996
Same start as The Monk and The Nun, but traverse further right for the start of this line. The original belay was from there, but the anchor station was removed. If climbed from the bottom it is 10 bolts and more than 35m (!)						
46 The Monk	6a	★★★	35m	11 bolts	Sport	1996
Long classic route on nice holds to the top. Extend the first two bolts to reduce rope drag.						
47 The Nun	6a	★★★	30m	11 bolts	Sport	2009
Also a classic, extend the first clip and have a look at the Monk's cave halfway up to the left.						
48 Unnamed ✖	6a		20m	unknown	Trad	
Fixed anchor at the top. Nuts and cams for the crack. Starts on the left of the Monk's former walkway to his cave.						
49 Batman ✖	6c		15m	5 bolts	Sport	1997
Second pitch of route 48. Goes through the guano-filled big wide crack in the high roof, well above the Monk's cave.						
50 Face it! ✖	7c	★★	25m	unknown	Sport	2008
Challenging face climb some meters on the left of the Monk's cave.						

EIN FARA | STROLL SECTOR

STROLL SECTOR This sector is on the same wall, just a little stroll up the Wadi from Monk. The sector is comprised of only a few routes from easy ones to unclimbed projects. At the time of writing of this guidebook this sector was closed by the Israeli National Park Authority. Please check before climbing.

ROUTE	GRADE	RATING	METERS	BOLTS	STYLE	DEVELOPED
51 The Last Mohican ✘	project		25m	unknown		2010
First route on the right. Looks pretty hard.						
52 Shmeltzy-heee? ✘	project		25m	unknown		2010
Second from the right. Looks hard too.						
53 Gemini ✘	6c+	★★	25m	unknown		2010
Face climbing. Shares the first bolts with Stroll.						
54 Stroll ✘	6a	★	30m	unknown		2007
Start on the small crack and then traverse to the left to finish on the vertical face.						
55 Lucky Strike ✘	6b+	★★	30m	unknown		2007
Long face climbing.						
56 Stroll Direct ✘	6c+		28m	unknown		2007
Hard version of Stroll. Last bolts and the station are shared with Stroll (54).						
57 Unnamed ✘	5b/5c			unknown		2008
Short slab slightly farther from the Stroll sector. Walk about 5 minutes past Stroll Direct (56).						

Ben Korff fueled by fresh goat milk on "Boulder Express," 7c+ (undisclosed location)
Photo by Dario Franchetti

AFRICA SECTOR | EIN FARAH

AFRICA SECTOR It is located across the wadi from the Ventilator Sector (Southern Wall) and west of Stroll Sector. It is reachable both from the bottom of the valley, passing Jeremiah, Pigs in Space, Monk, and Stroll Sectors (5 min. walking from Stroll), and from the Southern Wall, crossing the canyon. Due to its exposure, it is mostly a winter climbing area. At time of research, this sector was closed by the parks authority. Please check before climbing.

ROUTE	GRADE	RATING	METERS	BOLTS	STYLE	DEVELOPED
58 The Perfect Boulder ✖	project			Top-rope	Boulder	
There are two bolts on the top to set up a top-rope for this "Perfect Boulder".						
59 Soup of the Day ✖	6c	★	20m	unknown	Sport	1998
Overhanging start and then face with sharp holds.						
60 Carlsbad ✖	6a+	★★	30m	unknown	Trad	2007
Take big tricams. Start on the right of the small cave and continue up, slightly right, along the crack towards the big bush. Then a short slab and another crack leading to the final chimney. Top out over the chockstone. No station.						
61 Madagascar ✖	5b/5c		30m	unknown	Trad	2007
Easy but badly protected. Start on the crack on the right side of pillar until you reach a small cave. Continue up-left and top-out. No station.						
62 The Nile ✖	5b/5c		30m	unknown	Trad	2007
Start in the middle of the pillar, using the horizontal cracks, then link up with Madagascar (61). No station.						
63 Ivory Coast ✖	4+	★★	30m	unknown	Trad	
Climb on the left side of the pillar and follow the crack to the end of the face. Same top-out as for The Nile (62). Well protected. No station.						
64 Shock ✖	5c			unknown	Sport	1998
Short face climb.						
65 Jibril Rajub ✖	7a+			unknown	Sport	
100m left of Shock (64). It starts on the right of the right wall of the overhanging.						

EIN FARA | POKEMON SECTOR

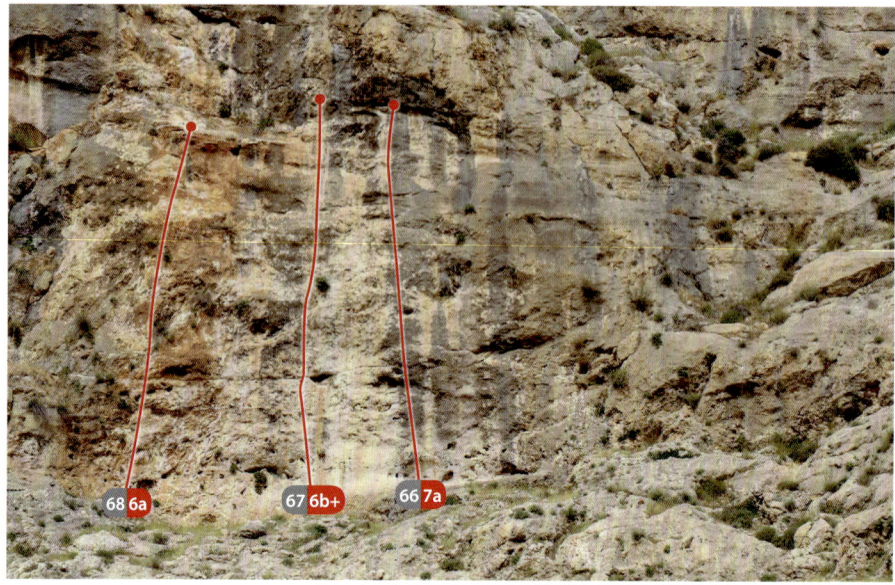

POKEMON SECTOR The Sector is situated after the Africa and in front of the Ventilator Sector (Southern Wall). It is exposed to the East and has sun in the summer until 15:00 and shade in the winter. It is composed of only three routes. At time of research, this sector was closed by the parks authority. Please check before climbing.

ROUTE	GRADE	RATING	METERS	BOLTS	STYLE	DEVELOPED
66 Unnamed ✖ Careful: badly bolted! Face climbing.	7a		15m	unknown	Sport	1997
67 Unnamed ✖ Face climbing.	6b+	★★★	15m	unknown	Sport	1997
68 Unnamed ✖ Face climbing.	6a		15m	unknown	Sport	1997

SOUTHERN WALL | EIN FARAH

Ben Korff on "Dvivon," 7c (page 108)
Photo by unknown

SOUTHERN WALL Ein Fara's Southern Wall offers a variety of interesting routes, from easy 5s to very hard 7s. Each sector has a different angle of exposure, so you can find shade/sun all day. It is thus well climbable all year round. The area is comprised of four sectors: Academy, Ventilator, Balcony, and Up The Valley. Most of the harder routes (and afternoon shade) can be found in the Academy sector. Ventilator and Balcony offer a number of warm-up routes, but also some harder stuff (and shade in the morning).

The Southern Wall is located outside the payment area of the Israeli Nature Reserve (see the Access section at the beginning of this chapter), and it is possible to climb after the daily closure time of the Nature Reserve (if you park your car outside the Almon Settlement). Note that the Israel Nature and Parks Authority is currently not permitting climbing in Up The Valley Sector.

EIN FARA | ACADEMY SECTOR

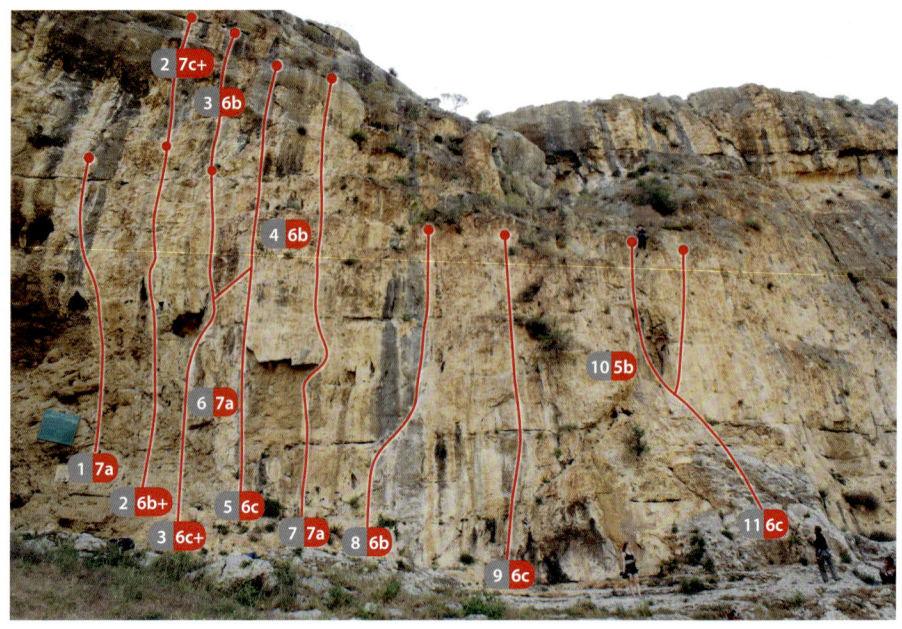

ACADEMY SECTOR LEFT SIDE Shade around noon and most of the medium-hard routes of the Southern Wall are found here. Mainly face and pumpy overhanging climbing.

ROUTE	GRADE	RATING	METERS	BOLTS	STYLE	DEVELOPED
1 Butcher's Chunk	7a	★★	21m	7 bolts	Sport	2011
The first route after the big cave, directly to the right of the big sign.						
2 Beef Shoulder	6b+	★★★	21m	8 bolts	Sport	2009
Very nice, juggy, sustained and overhanging classic.						
Beef Shoulder – Pitch 2	7c+		12m	5 bolts	Sport	
Can be climbed in one go from the ground; take a long rope (70m). Five additional bolts counting the station of pitch 1. Better climbed as second pitch (rope drag).						
3 Border Run	6c+	★★	21m	7 bolts	Sport	2008
Another nice line. Cruxy after the cave and delicate before the station. Great length if combined with the second pitch.						
Border Run – Pitch 2	6b	★	12m	6 bolts	Sport	
Series of long moves, pumpy and juggy. Can be climbed in one go with a 70m rope; 6 additional bolts counting the station.						
4 Variation to Border Run (3)	6b	★★	27m	unknown	Sport	
Links the start of Border Run with the top of Shades of Beauty to avoid the harder section of either route. Climb until the cave, clip the next bolt, and then traverse to the right to link up with Shades of Beauty.						

ROUTE	GRADE	RATING	METERS	BOLTS	STYLE	DEVELOPED
5 Shades of Beauty	6c	★	27m	unknown	Sport	2006

Pumpy at the start, balance-y at the top.

6 Variation to Shades of B. (6)	7a	★★		unknown	Sport	

Start on Shades of Beauty and then traverse left above the cave to link up with Border Run to the top.

7 Dr. Evil & Mr. Hyde	7a		27m	8 bolts	Sport	2006

Interesting moves around the overhang (careful at the third clip).

8 Spaced Out	6b	★	14m	4 bolts	Sport	2007

Nice line. Careful between the second and third clip.

9 Northern Wind	6c	★	16m	8 bolts	Sport	

Short and boulder-y.

10 Bomba	5b		18m	6 bolts	Sport	2007

Short warm-up route to the left of the cave.

11 Pompa	6c		17m	5 bolts	Sport	2007

Starts as Bomba, but then to the right of the cave. A few delicate moves on the face.

Miranda Oakley on "Butcher's Chunk," 7a (page 104)
Photo by Markus Maier

EIN FARA | ACADEMY SECTOR

ROUTE	GRADE	RATING	METERS	BOLTS	STYLE	DEVELOPED
12 Middleman	6b+	★	19m	7 bolts	Sport	2006

Better than it looks. Some nice physical moves between the 2nd and the 4th bolt.

13 Spare the Rod, Spoil the Route	6a	★★	27m	9 bolts	Sport	2006

Long warm-up with hard-ish section in the beginning. Cruxy and a few polished layback moves.

14 Jamming in the Holy Land	6c		27m	unknown	Trad	

Trad line along the obvious crack. Use anchor of Spare the Rod. Lose rock and tricky gear placements.

15 Unnamed	6a		24m	unknown	Trad	

Climb along the crack via the small pillar to the bolted station of 140$ (16). Good protection with small and medium nuts and cams.

16 140$	7a	★★	23m	9 bolts	Sport	2006

Worth the money—sustained on small crimps and pockets. First route on the right of the trad crack.

17 Pain in the Ass	7a+	★★	25m	9 bolts	Sport	2006

Reach-y start, a traverse to the left (after second bolt) and then delicate and sustained climbing to the top.

18 Yonatan Shapiro	7b+	★★	25m	8 bolts	Sport	2007

Shares the first two (or three) bolts with Pain in the Ass. Reach-y start to delicate moves on small holds up the black stripe. Named after a former Israeli Air Force Pilot, now a peace activist.

19 Sometimes Difficult Never Impossible	7c+		21m	unknown	Sport	

More like: very difficult, almost impossible. Hard for the grade.

Tim Bruns on "Yonatan Shapiro," 7b+ (page 106)
Photo by Dario Franchetti

EIN FARA | ACADEMY SECTOR

ROUTE	GRADE	RATING	METERS	BOLTS	STYLE	DEVELOPED
20 Dvivon (Racoon)	7c	★★	18m	9 bolts	Sport	2009

Physical start. Further up, when holds are disappearing, either do the evasive maneuver to the right before coming back in line for the little overhang, or alternatively continue straight up to the station (a little harder). Careful on that mono!

21 King of Vafanculo	7c+	★★	20m	6 bolts	Sport	2010

Intense line, a bit spaced out towards the end due to lack of holds to clip from...

22 Mixta Grill	7b+		12m	4 bolts	Sport	1998

Variety of moves on somewhat polished holds.

Extension to Mixta Grill (22)	7b+			0 bolts	Sport	

Continue straight up after Mixta Grill's (22) anchor, before moving left to finish on Vafanculo's anchor (21). Bouldery. Doesn't make the route any harder or nicer.

23 A0 Approach	A0		10m	5 bolts	Aid	

Short A0-assisted climb to get to the anchor for the 5 routes to the right of Mixta Grill (22). Clip and use the rope to pull yourself up. This and all the routes on top are rarely climbed. Take a 70 meters rope if you want to rappel directly to the ground from the station of the next 5 routes (24, 25, 26, 27, 28).

24 Jeans Butt	5c		25m	8 bolts	Sport	

From the A0 station, traverse left, choose your clips wisely, and follow the thorny bushes far up through the main crack/chimney. Station is located after the little overhang.

25 Arik is Thinking About It	6c+		25m	8 bolts	Sport	

From the A0 station, almost straight up. Easy start, hard at the overhang. Originally graded as 6a+.

ACADEMY SECTOR | EIN FARAH

ROUTE	GRADE	RATING	METERS	BOLTS	STYLE	DEVELOPED
26 Rotor	6b	★★	25m	8 bolts	Sport	

From the A0 station, traverse to the right and then go straight up before the little bush. Very nice moves, but a bit runout with multi-pitch feel.

27 Divergence	6b	★★	25m	6 bolts	Sport	

From the A0 anchor traverse far right, past Rotor and take the next line straight up. Nice, but scary since bolts are well spaced out. Careful when you pull the rope (there is a little flake where it can get stuck)!

ROUTE	GRADE	RATING	METERS	BOLTS	STYLE	DEVELOPED
28 Convergence	6b		25m	7 bolts	Sport	

Links Divergence with the top of Islands in the Stream. Shares the first three bolts with Divergence, links up to the intermediate station of Islands in the Stream and continues up two more bolts to the higher station.

29 Islands in the Stream	7c+	★★★	22m	9 bolts	Sport	2007

Pumpy and continuous. One of the best lines in the valley.

30 Diagonal	6c+	★	30m	5 bolts	Sport	

Strongly right-traversing line. Somewhat polished. The station is high behind the shrubbery.

31 Kal Kar	6a		15m	4 bolts	Sport	2007

Rarely climbed. First pitch to reach The Tomb. The anchor is above the little tree. Beware of loose rock.

EIN FARA | ACADEMY SECTOR

ROUTE	GRADE	RATING	METERS	BOLTS	STYLE	DEVELOPED
32 The Tomb	6c	★	21m	7 bolts	Sport	2007

If you like it a bit rough and to escape the crowds, try this slightly overhanging, sharp and crumbly chimney. Use Kal Kar (31) as first pitch and then carefully(!) scramble up to the right to the obvious crack/chimney.

| 33 Natif for the Poor | 7a | ★★ | 12m | 5 bolts | Sport | 2007 |

Powerful, reachy overhang followed by interesting face climbing. Less slippery than it looks.

| 34 The Prophecy | 7a+ | | 12m | 5 bolts | Sport | 2008 |

Short roof route with long and physical moves. *Inshallah* (God willing) the horizontal bridge stays strong.

| 35 Dirty Peter | 7a+/7b | | 26m | unknown | Sport | 2011 |

Overhanging start through a small roof.

110

Tawfiq Nada climbing in the Academy Sector
Photo by Miranda Oakley

EIN FARA | VENTILATOR SECTOR

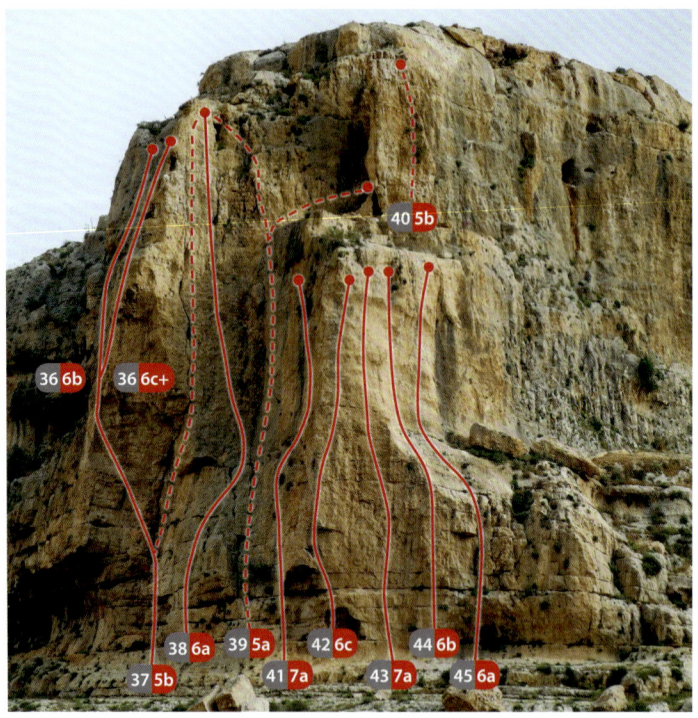

VENTILATOR Small and well-ventilated sector at the corner with an interesting variety of routes as well as a few trad options. Routes 36-41 are shady in the afternoon, while 42-45 are shady in the morning.

ROUTE	GRADE	RATING	METERS	BOLTS	STYLE	DEVELOPED
36 Adi's Doctorate	6c+	★★	27m	12 bolts	Sport	2007

Mediocre rock quality up to the corner, but then a nice and exposed climb up the face. Extend bolts 3 and 7 if you can to reduce rope drag. Clip either bolt 4 or bolt 5.

Variation to Adi's Doctorate (36)	6b	★	28m	12 bolts	Sport	

Links Adi's Doctorate to Dirty Peter (35), avoiding the hard sections of either. Follow Adi's Doctorate until bolt 7 then stay somewhat on the left. Consider skipping bolts 4 and 8 to reduce rope drag - or extend them well.

37 Traditional Modern Times	5b	★★	30m	unknown	Trad	

Start in the obvious crack (mind loose rocks). Continue on to the face close to the left edge till the top. Use the anchor of Modern Times. Small and medium nuts, tricams and friends. Good protection.

38 Modern Times	6a	★★★	32m	10 bolts	Sport	2006

Nice, long, classic, and still sharp. Easy for the grade. A recent addition of more bolts has made it less runout.

VENTILATOR SECTOR | EIN FARAH

ROUTE	GRADE	RATING	METERS	BOLTS	STYLE	DEVELOPED
39 Corner Crack	5a	★★	27m		Trad	

Follow the obvious crack and top-out on the big ledge. You will find an improvised station made of a fixed rope and a maillon at the base of the pillar. Small and medium trad gear, good protection. Alternately you can finish at the station of Modern Times.

40 Pillar	5b	★	10m		Trad	2006

Second pitch of Corner Crack. The station of route 39 is on the left side of the Pillar, but the best ascent to the top is from the right side. We recommend moving around the pillar (stay on belay) and then build your own station on the right side (you only need one long sling). The pillar does not offer much gear placements. On the top you will find an anchor made of a fixed rope and a maillon. Descend the same way you came.

41 One Move Wonder	7a		21m	8 bolts	Sport	2006

The name says it all.

42 The Corner	6c	★★★	20m	8 bolts	Sport	1995

Physical start, then delicate balancing left and right of the corner. Rebolted in 2006.

43 The Crying Game	7a	★★	20m	7 bolts	Sport	2012

Engaging face and slab climb.

44 Ventilator	6b	★★★	20m	7 bolts	Sport	1995

Great climb, interesting moves. Rebolted in 2006.

45 Ambicioso	6a	★★	21m	8 bolts	Sport	1995

Rebolted in 2006.

Urwah Askar on "Ambicioso," 6a (page 113)
Photo by Ray Wood

EIN FARA | BALCONY SECTOR

BALCONY A number of mainly beginner's and warm-up routes on an elevated rock ledge. Scramble up at the end of Ventilator Sector. Shade in summer until midday. Mostly sunny in winter.

ROUTE	GRADE	RATING	METERS	BOLTS	STYLE	DEVELOPED
46 Testa Rossa	5c	★★	26m	11 bolts	Sport	2010
First route on the very left of the balcony. A bit tricky and a little run out to reach the station—stay left.						
47 Peril Roja	5c		27m	11 bolts	Sport	2010
Second route on the left. Also tricky for the grade. There is a first anchor midway after 14m (5 bolts).						
48 Hanna Banana	5c		20m	8 bolts	Sport	2007
Good beginner's route. Starts with an easy scramble before becoming more vertical.						
49 70 kph	6a	★	28m	9 bolts	Sport	2007
Good warm-up. Easy start, a bit harder on the face - like most of the routes in this sector						
50 Hei Hop	5c	★★	25m	8 bolts	Sport	2009
Up to the cave, out to the right of it and then straight up. Interesting rock towards the end.						
51 Hamor Garem	6a+	★	25m	9 bolts	Sport	2009
Hardish crux for the grade.						
52 Flash the Goat Hunter	6b+	★★	20m	8 bolts	Sport	2007
Hold on tight on small crimps.						
53 Bim Bam Bam Tiras Ham	6b	★	20m	unknown	Sport	
Quite sustained climbing on small crimps. Hard for the grade.						

BALCONY SECTOR/ UP THE VALLEY | EIN FARAH

ROUTE	GRADE	RATING	METERS	BOLTS	STYLE	DEVELOPED
54 Not Hard but Spiky	6c	★★	20m	7 bolts	Sport	2007
Interesting moves on small sharp crimps.						
55 Im Kztat Pilpel Bayashvan	6b+	★	18m	9 bolts	Sport	
Small pockets and sharp crimps.						
56 Mr Panino	7a		18m	unknown	Sport	2011
Tricky on small holds.						
57 Organized Crime	7b		18m	unknown	Sport	2011
Similar to Mr Panino but harder.						
58 Hot & Dumb	6c		18m	6 bolts	Sport	2011
Last route on the right, just left of the sign. Easy start, quite tough after the band. Originally graded 6b.						

UP THE VALLEY At the time of writing of this guidebook this sector was closed by the Israeli National Park Authority. Please check before climbing.

ROUTE	GRADE	RATING	METERS	BOLTS	STYLE	DEVELOPED
59 Unnamed ✖	7a	★★	15m	unknown	Sport	1998
Scramble back down from the balcony and follow the little trail further up the valley. Starts inside the cave. Looks like the first few bolts have been removed.						
60 Unnamed ✖	7c			unknown	Sport	2009
Scramble up from route 59 to reach the start of this route.						

The following routes are located in the little sector with a nice face, which you pass when you hike down the long way. At the time of writing of this guidebook this sector was closed by the Israeli National Park Authority. Please check before climbing.

ROUTE	GRADE	RATING	METERS	BOLTS	STYLE	DEVELOPED
61 Unknown ✖	6c?			unknown	Sport	
Overhanging Corner						
62 Unknown ✖	8a?			unknown	Sport	
Crazy Face						
63 Unknown ✖	6a	★★	24m	7 bolts	Sport	
Very nice crack and chimney climb, a bit runout towards the end (don't fall!).						
64 Unknown ✖	7c?			unknown	Sport	
Face left						
65 Unknown ✖	7c?			unknown	Sport	
Face middle						
66 Unknown ✖	7c?			unknown	Sport	
Face right						

07 . BATTIR ★☆☆☆☆

07 BATTIR

Routes	29 (potential for more)
Length	10m
Rock	Limestone
Political Area	C
Coordinates	31.723103, 35.147768 (Green Cliff), 31.725422, 35.150656 (Yellow Cliff)

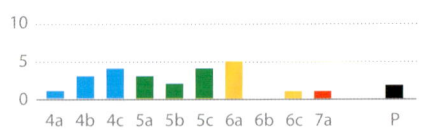

Sign showing the way from the access road
Photo by Acciareria

OVERVIEW

Until very recently, climbing in the West Bank was focused on the crags around Ramallah and the valleys leading towards the Jordan Valley. In Bethlehem, there are two climbing associations: PAMSD, supported by the French Alpine Club, and Laylac (situated in Dheisheh refugee camp), supported by Italian climbers. Laylac has a project called "Westclimbingbank," an initiative supported by Acciaieria, a climbing gym in Milan with a reputation for civil disobedience and alternative culture. In 2018, local and international climbers started developing some routes around the historic and picturesque village of Battir. Most of the routes are between 4a and 6a, which makes it an ideal spot for beginners. Battir is a very popular hiking area offering great views and a number of

Roman ruins and tombs. The village is also famous for an ancient democratic system of water distribution between the farmers. After a hot climbing day, you can find refreshments and much needed Palestinian food in one of several restaurants at the beginning of the hiking trail. Development of climbing around Battir has only just begun. Just a ten minutes' walk from the yellow cliff there are two big caves with potential for about 20 routes, some of them in harder grades. If you are an experienced route developer and keen to establish new lines, please contact us.

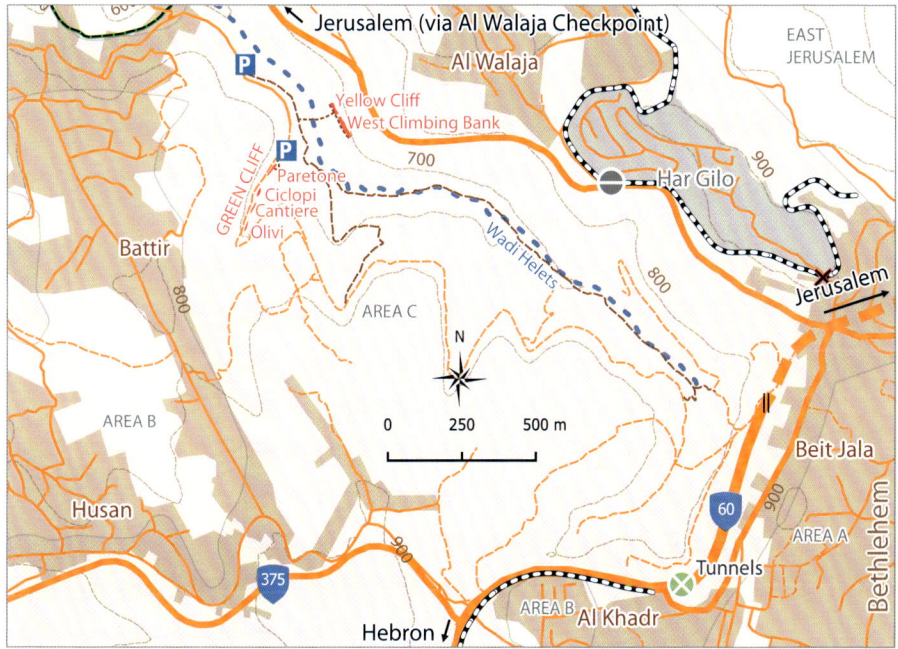

DIRECTIONS

By car: Drive to the village of Battir near Bethlehem, and follow the main street all the way down the hill to the old part of town. On the main street, you will pass the Roman pool and the Terrace Cafe Al Jenan restaurant (we recommend it!) on your left. Follow the main road. After 500 meters towards the village boundary it makes a slight right turn. Soon you will be greeted with a view of the Battir valley. Keep following that road, which slightly ascends the south side of the valley. You will pass a small wooden sign indicating a hiking trail that descends into the valley to your left (there are some so-called Roman carpenter ruins to be marveled at). After driving for another couple of hundred meters you finally arrive at the "parking spot" on the left-hand side of the road (basically a widened stretch of the road – check the coordinates). To reach the green cliff, catch a trail

BATTIR

descending just a couple of meters down from the road to the wall. For the yellow cliff, you descend the same way, hike further through olive trees down to the valley floor and go up to the opposite (northern) valley wall. Improvise for the exact route as there is no dedicated trail. (Use GPS coordinates for precise location.)

By public transport: Take public transport from Ramallah to Bethlehem (1 to 2 hours). Once in Bethlehem, take a shared taxi to a location called 'cinema'. From there, take another service (shared taxi) to Battir village. At the final stop, walk along the main road and follow the instructions above.

CRAG DEVELOPERS

Laylac & Acciaieria (Westclimbingbank), Inas Radaydeh, Moritz Schendel, and Matthias Wurtenberger.

Photo by Markus Maier

GREEN CLIFF | BATTIR

PARETONE / CENTRAL SECTOR

ROUTE	GRADE	RATING	METERS	BOLTS	STYLE	DEVELOPED
1 Motaz	4b		9m	3 bolts & 1 sling	Sport	2018
Nice, easy but exposed warm-up climb with great holds.						
2 Raed	4c		9m	3 bolts & 2 slings	Sport	2018
Start in between two boulders as you move up.						
3 Falastin	5a		9m	4 bolts	Sport	2018
The bolters wanted to keep you super safe so you will find a bolt at every step.						
4 Nasheet Qamr	5c		9m	4 bolts	Sport	2018
Stay on the face all the way, and don't escape to the right where the climb turns to a 5a. Appreciate the bolters who finished the route in bright moonlight.						
5 Hyena	6a		10m	3 bolts	Sport	2018
Sometimes one can hear hyenas in the valley of Battir, especially at night.						
6 Unnamed	P			No bolts	Only top-rope	2018
If taking the overhang, otherwise 4c.						
7. Areda	5b		9m	5 bolts	Sport	2018
A left heelhook will get you sorted at the crux of the route.						
8. Seba	5c+		9m	3 bolts	Sport	2018
Find the good hold for clipping the 3rd bolt, the rest is a walk in the park.						

BATTIR | GREEN CLIFF

CICLOPI/THREE CYCLOPS SECTOR
This sector is a couple of meters left of Paretone Sector and features pumpy routes in the overhang. Definitely a highlight in Battir.

ROUTE	GRADE	RATING	METERS	BOLTS	STYLE	DEVELOPED
9 Shajara	6a+		8m	4 bolts	Sport	2018
Go straight for the big hole as you enjoy this boulder-style route.						
10 Jumana's Smile	6a+		8m	4 bolts	Sport	2018
Pumpy route, you can either go for the crack on the left or search for small holds straight up.						
11 Hajiz/Checkpoint	7a		10m	3 bolts	Sport	2018
The lousy finger pocket at the crux in the overhang will keep you in check.						

GREEN CLIFF | BATTIR

CANTIERE/DOCKYARD SECTOR
Here only one route has been bolted, several others are awaiting brave bolters and strong climbers.

ROUTE	GRADE	RATING	METERS	BOLTS	STYLE	DEVELOPED
12 Better Nate Than Lever Crimpy crux.	6c		10m	3 bolts	Sport	2018

BATTIR | GREEN CLIFF

ULIVI/BABY SECTOR
This sector is perfect for beginners, kids, and those who want to learn how to lead.

ROUTE	GRADE	RATING	METERS	BOLTS	STYLE	DEVELOPED
13 Tofah	4b		8m	4bolts	Sport	2018
The first route as you approach the cliff from below and the easiest.						
14 Momtaa	4c		8m	3 bolt	Sport	2018
You will need to do a sidepull at the anchor.						
15 Kalamantena	4a		8m	3 bolts	Sport	2018
16 Al Quds	5a		9m	5 bolts	Sport	2018
The hardest route in this sector, crimps with nice feet placements.						
17 Moza	4c+		7m	3 bolts	Sport	2018
Shares last bolt and anchor with Al Quds (16).						

YELLOW CLIFF | BATTIR

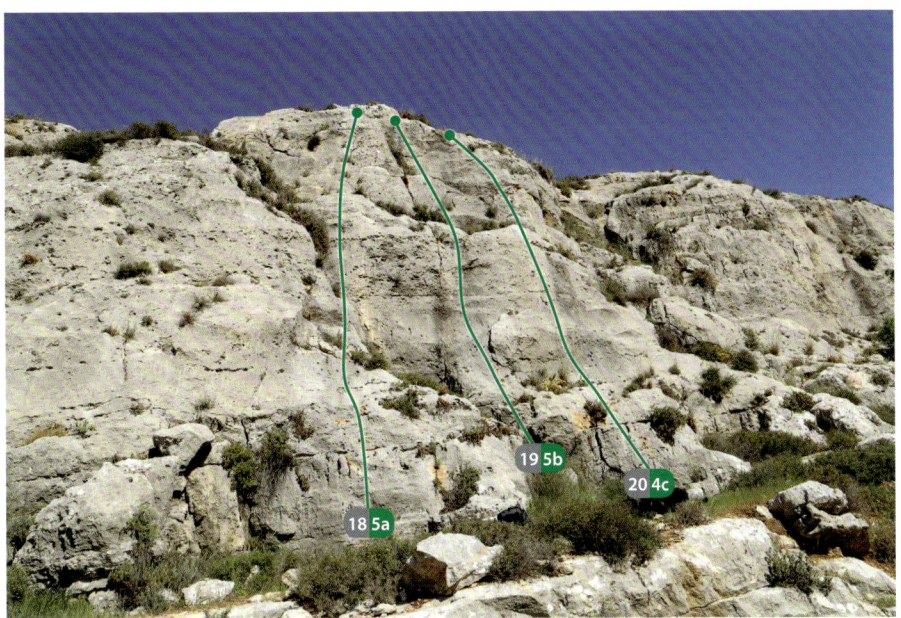

The following crags are located directly opposite the Green Cliff on the other side of the valley. To access these cliffs, traverse the valley floor to the north from the Green Cliff.

YELLOW CLIFF
The first sector as you walk from Battir was bolted in 2017 by French climbers.

ROUTE	GRADE	RATING	METERS	BOLTS	STYLE	DEVELOPED
18 No Name	5a	★	11m	4 bolts	Sport	2018
19 Jehad J.	5b	★★	11m	4 bolts	Sport	2018
20 Walking in Sunshine	4c	★	11m		Sport	2018

BATTIR | YELLOW CLIFF

WEST CLIMBING BANK
This crag is next to the Yellow Cliff, about a 10-minute walk from the Green Cliff. The steep limestone walls offer easy routes on compact limestone. Nine routes and one project have been established.

ROUTE	GRADE	RATING	METERS	BOLTS	STYLE	DEVELOPED
21 Alm Falastin	P		10m	3 bolts	Sport	2018
22 Asal/Honey Tough start and long runout at the end.	5b		10m	3 bolts	Sport	2018
23 Wade Great chips to hold on to.	5a		10m	3 bolts	Sport	2018
24 Kalb/Heart Shares style and anchor station with Wade (23).	4b		10m	3 bolts	Sport	2018
25 Sakher Shares an anchor with Moftah Alawda (26).	4c		10m	3 bolts	Sport	2018
26 Moftah Alawda Tough slabs at the beginning, the rest is easy.	6a		10m	3 bolts	Sport	2018

YELLOW CLIFF | BATTIR

ROUTE	GRADE	RATING	METERS	BOLTS	STYLE	DEVELOPED
27 Farasha/Butterfly Move like a butterfly.	5c		12m	5 bolts	Sport	2018
28 Bater A lot of smearing to do, halfway up swing left to get key hold.	5c		10m	3 bolts	Sport	2018
29 Warda/Flower Go up in a zigzag.	6a		10m	4 bolts	Sport	2018

An undeveloped cliff with potential, featuring a nice overhang, can be found off to the left when walking up the valley. If you want to check it out, follow the trail to the Yellow Cliff and proceed further for another kilometer or so.

Battir offers marvelous views across the valley
Photo by Acciareria

08 . WADI TAMER ★★★★★

08 WADI TAMER

Routes	11 + 15 Boulders
Length	15-35m
Rock	Limestone
Political Area	C
Coordinates	31.63962 N, 35.41307 E

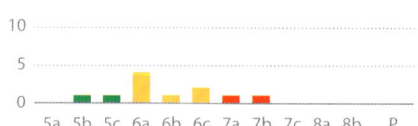

OVERVIEW
Wadi Tamer is a small, remote climbing area located a few hundred meters from the western shores of the Dead Sea. What it lacks in quality rock climbing, it makes up for with rugged desert vibes and views across the Dead Sea to Jordan. The rock quality here is questionable at best, and the fact that most of the climbs ascend a dry waterfall from seasonal flooding means that the rock is usually coated in sand and debris. This is also one of the only areas in Palestine that offers multi-pitch traditional climbing.

SEASON
As Wadi Tamer is located roughly 450 meters below sea level, the only reasonable time to climb here is during the cooler winter months. During the summer, it is unbearably hot. That being said, during winter, be aware of the weather because rain at higher altitudes does mean flash flooding in Wadi Tamer! So, check the local weather forecast on the day of your climb!

WADI TAMER

GEAR
The routes here are a mix of sport and traditional climbs. Many of the bolts and anchor stations situated on the face of the dry waterfall have been smashed or warped by falling rocks during periods of flash floods. The trad placements are often creative and sketchy. Wearing a helmet is an absolute must! Be prepared for anything!

DIRECTIONS
From Jerusalem (1-1.5 hours by car): Leave the city through the Al Zaim checkpoint heading east on Route 1 towards the Dead Sea. Once past Jericho, continue south on Route 90 along the Dead Sea. At the T-intersection with a gas station on your right, take a right following the sign towards Qumran, Kalia, Ein Gedi. From this intersection drive roughly 17 km (10-15 minutes) and you will see Wadi Tamer on your right. There are a number of canyon washes descending the large east-facing cliffs on your right. Use the GPS coordinates provided to make sure you are at the right place. Park on the eastern side of the road just at the entrance to an Israeli settlement date farm. The coordinates for the parking are 31.639261N, 35.417942E. By foot, cross the road and hike up the wash following a trail marked by white-green stripes to reach the cliff. The boulder blocs are located before the Waterfall sector on the right side of the path.

DIRECTIONS
From Ramallah (1.5 hours by car): Take the main Jerusalem Road south from Ramallah, passing the Qalandia refugee camp on your left and the Qalandia checkpoint on your right. Continue southeast past Al–Ram until you reach the Jaba'a junction at which you take a sharp right onto road 437. Follow

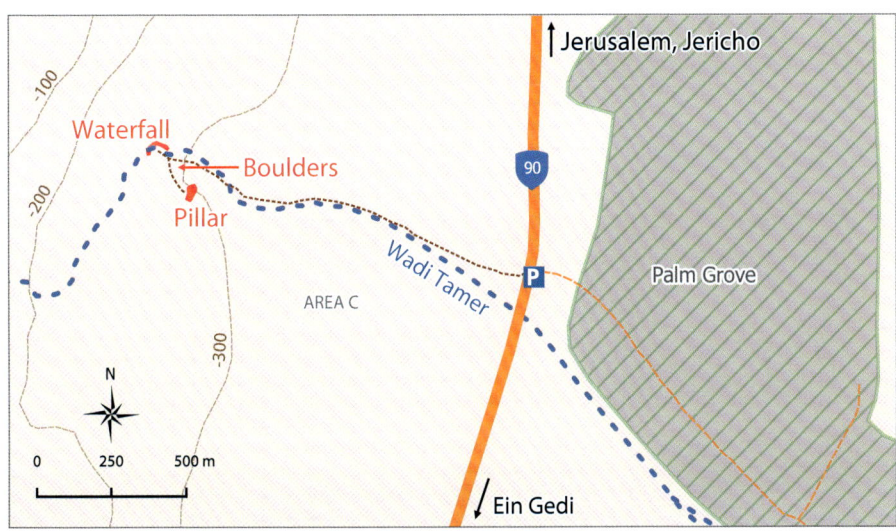

WADI TAMER

the road past the village of Hizma until it runs into Route 1. Take a left and head east, descending into the Jordan valley. From there on, follow the description above.

CONFLICT

Wadi Tamer is located in a part of the West Bank rarely visited by Palestinians. The fact that Route 90 dead-ends in a checkpoint to the south means that there are few reasons for Palestinians to travel that way. Wadi Tamer is accessible for Palestinians, but bear in mind that a green-plated Palestinian car could arouse some suspicion in this area.

OTHER ACTIVITIES

A trip to Wadi Tamer could easily be combined with a visit to the Dead Sea and/or Jericho. Be aware that it is not safe or legal to swim in the Dead Sea outside of an established beach. To avoid trouble, it is better to visit and pay the entrance fee at one of the designated beaches like Kalia Beach resort. Kalia Beach and other resorts are Israeli-owned businesses and constitute illegal settlements in the West Bank. Despite that, many of the visitors to Kalia Beach are local Palestinians from Jericho.

CRAG DEVELOPERS

The crag was developed by Israeli climbers. Gil Aberbauch opened the boulders.

Tyler Myers on "Unnamed (7)," 7a+ (page 129)
Photo by Matthias Wurtenberger

THE WATERFALL | WADI TAMER

THE WATERFALL

ROUTE	GRADE	RATING	METERS	BOLTS	STYLE	DEVELOPED
1 Waterfall (easy start)	6a	★★★	27/45m	0 bolts	trad	

Start at the left crack and then join the classic waterfall route. You can either abseil from the bolted anchor (featuring 2 maillons) on the small ledge or continue climbing the second pitch. There is not a lot of protection in the second pitch, bring small nuts or tricams. From the top anchor the abseil is 45 meters, thus you will need to build a station in between.

2 Waterfall (hard start)	7b	★	27/45m	4 bolts	Mixed	

Use the bolts until you join the main crack of the classic waterfall route.

3 The Classic Waterfall Route	6a+	★★★	45m	0 bolts	trad	

Physical start, but great fun!

4 Offwidth	6c+	★	45m	0 bolts	trad	

As the name suggests, pack some larger cams. At the end of the offwidth crack, traverse left to join the Waterfall route and rappel from its anchor (2 maillons).

5 Fist Line	6a+	★★	18m	6 bolts	trad	

Tough beginning, use your fists and bring large cams or you're doomed.

6 Cave Line	6c+		18m	0 bolts	trad	

Starts on the left side of the cave. Use the anchor of Fist Line.

7 Unnamed	7a+	★	21m	10 bolts	Sport	

Tough and sandy.

8 Unnamed	5b	★★	20 meters	6 bolts		

Scenic climbing up the exposed corner.

WADI TAMER | THE PILLAR

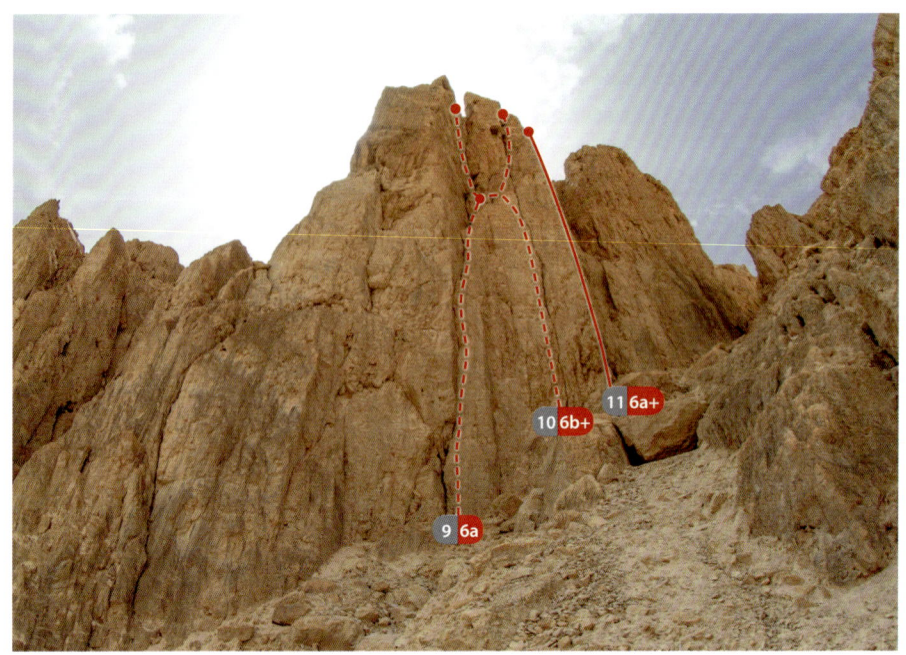

THE PILLAR

ROUTE	GRADE	RATING	METERS	BOLTS	STYLE	DEVELOPED
9 The Pillar (left)	6a	★★★	35/45m	1 bolts	trad	

There is one bolt at the beginning to protect the start (and the belayer).
For most of the time, you are climbing a small crack, so bring small cams and nuts.

	Pitch 2 a)	5c		10m			

Follow the dihedral to the left. Ends at a bolted anchor, offering great views on the valley

	Pitch 2 b)	5c		10m			

Follow the crack to the right. Once you reach the top plateau descend to the left to the bolted anchor (be careful). From the top anchor you need can either abseil to the ground (if your double-rope is longer than 45m) or abseil to the lower anchor and then to the ground.

10 The Pillar (right)	6b+	★★	28m	0 bolts	trad	

Gear can be tricky to place. You will need cams and tricams.

11 Unnamed	6a+		35m	12 bolts	Sport	2018

Newly bolted route. Exposed climbing along the southwest corner. Plenty of loose rock – really take care here! Anchor is equipped with 2 maillons. Currently first bolt is missing, place a cam instead. Also cam friend for belayer.

Matthias Wurtenberger on "The Classic Waterfall Route," 6a+ (page 129)
Photo by Markus Maier

WADI TAMER BOULDERING

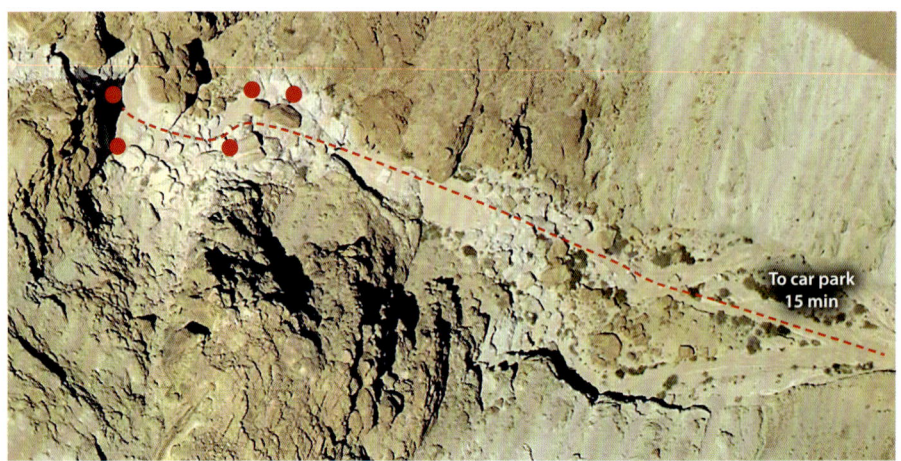

BOULDERING | WADI TAMER

ROUTE	GRADE
1 Sababasta	V4

Start on the left and traverse all the way to right. At the corner move up.

ROUTE	GRADE
2 Unnamed	V6

Climb towards the horizontal crack and then top out left.

| 3 Unnamed | V5 |

Start where the small crack begins, inside the cave. Follow the horizontal crack to the left and top out left around the corner.

WADI TAMER | BOULDERING

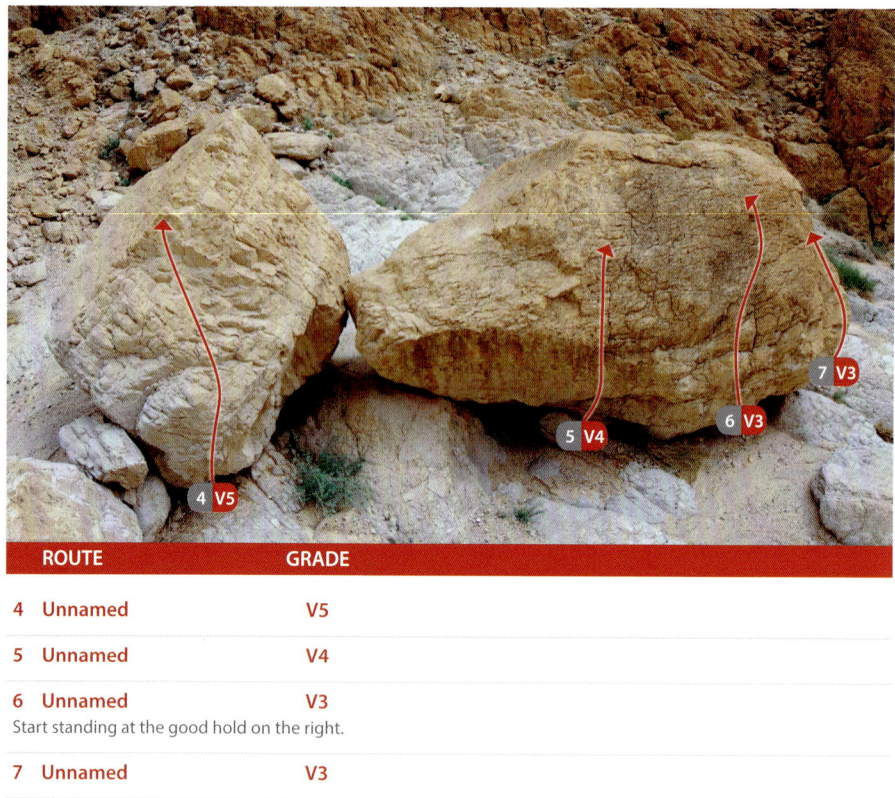

ROUTE	GRADE
4 Unnamed	V5
5 Unnamed	V4
6 Unnamed	V3

Start standing at the good hold on the right.

7 Unnamed	V3

BOULDERING | WADI TAMER

ROUTE	GRADE

8 Israeli Tamer V10
Use the undercling and the small crimp in the overhang to start.

9 Unnamed V5
Start at the big crack.

10 Unnamed V2

11 Unnamed V2

WADI TAMER | BOULDERING

ROUTE	GRADE
12 Solid Dude Climb up the arrete.	V6
13 Unnamed Start standing.	V3
14 Unnamed Climb to the left.	V4
15 Unnamed Climb straight up.	V5
16 Nice Dude	V6

View from the Pillar down to the boulders
Photo by Marcin Pius

09 NABLUS

Routes	18 (potential for 40)
Length	32m
Rock	Limestone
Political Area	A
Coordinates	32.228703, 35.264641

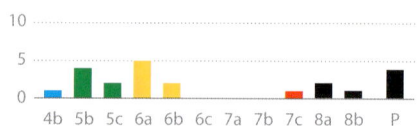

Wahid Masri instructing local kids before their first climb
Photo by Matthias Wurtenberger

OVERVIEW

The Nablus cliff is a truly unique climbing spot. Towering above the ancient city of Nablus, with its 300,000 inhabitants, it can be seen from nearly everywhere in the city. The rock is subject to many legends, particularly the one of "Al-Sitt Salimieh," a faithful female warrior who fought in Saladin's army. According to the legend, she was buried on top of the mountain above the cliff. Other stories tell of a witch who used a coffin as her mode of transport. While passing over Nablus, something went wrong and she crashed into the cliff and has been trapped there ever since. We haven't encountered her yet during the development of the crag, but better watch out! On a serious note, being on alert at the cliff is generally a good idea since it is a new cliff under development, and there is still a lot of loose rock. Wearing a helmet is an absolute must! The crag is very close to the city, and therefore you will usually find a lot of curious kids coming up to watch you climb. Make sure they are out of the rock-fall zone. If you have a kid's harness and a small helmet, let them have a try as well! So far, some have been given some top-rope practice by us.

With a height of 30 meters, Sid Slamieh is taller than the crags around Ramallah. The routes are beautiful but sometimes sharp. In general, we recommend using a 70-meter rope and 12 quickdraws.

The cliff is in the declared Area A (According to the Oslo Accords in 1994) and thereby under the authority of the PA. However, just a bit up the hill, situated on the peak of the mountain, is one of the most important Israeli intelligence surveillance stations. Thus, make sure not to walk around the cliff or hike up the mountain. Under no circumstances should you go close to the military base; that would be dangerous and ill-advised. Also, do not stay at the cliff past dark, as military patrols are known to pass by during the night. Nonetheless, we highly recommend staying to watch the sun set over the city to the sound of calming evening prayers—a truly spectacular sight!

Crag Developers
Wahid Masri, Markus Maier, Inas Radaydeh, Philipp Zwehl, Matthias Wurtenberger, Michael Schreiber, Tim Bruns, and Naturfreunde Nuremberg.

Markus rappelling to bolt the first anchor on what would become "Redemption at Last," 6a+ (page 142) in the summer of 2018
Photo by Matthias Wurtenberger

NABLUS

DIRECTIONS

By car: To access the cliff, you will need to drive through much of Nablus with its confusing, winding streets. As such, it is best to put the GPS coordinates into your navigation application and follow the directions. As a point of orientation and halfway mark, the point from which you will have to leave the main road dissecting Nablus from East to West in order to drive up the hill is the following: 32.215388, 35.27369. Park on the side of the road, just beneath the cliff. You can either directly scramble up the steep slope to the crag or walk through the parking space under the building directly in front of the rock. After you pass the parking, you will find some rather improvised stairs that pass by the neighboring houses. Walk up these stairs and then walk left towards the crag.

By public transport: From Ramallah, take a service (yellow shared mini bus) to Nablus. From the service station in Nablus, walk directly uphill to the north; you will have the cliff in view most of the way. Although relatively close to the center, be mindful of the fact that the walk from downtown to the climbing area requires several hundred meters of elevation gain.

Matthias Wurtenberger descending from a day of bolting and cleaning new routes
Photo by Tim Bruns

NABLUS | RIGHT

RIGHT

ROUTE	GRADE	RATING	METERS	BOLTS	STYLE	Developed
1 Don't Falafall	5c	★★	17m	5 bolts	Sport	2018
Don't let your weakness show on this route as the local kids watch you ascend.						
2 Yalla Yalla	6a		15m	5 bolts	Sport	2019
Tough start, once past the second bolt—yallah!						
3 Patience Palestine	5b	★	22m	5 bolts	Sport	2019
Long relaxed climb. Start in the wide crack so that you don't miss the first bolt which hides in it.						
4 Aibtisama	5c	★	20m	5 bolts	Sport	2019
Stick to the edge, good to place some heel-hooks. After the last bolt, leave the edge and head straight up to avoid risky traverse to the anchor. Shares the first two bolts as well as the anchor with Nice and Uncomplicated (5).						
5 Nice and Uncomplicated	5b	★	20m	6 bolts	Sport	2019
Nice crack climbing. If you climb the face instead, the route turns into a 5c.						
6 Redemption At Last	6a+	★★	21m	6 bolts	Sport	2018
This was the first route bolted in Nablus. Due to some complications with the drill battery, they didn't finish until late. Wahid Masri and Matthias Wurtenberger woke up at 5:00 the next morning and drove from Ramallah just to do the FA before Wahid caught a flight to the US later that day.						

MIDDLE | NABLUS

MIDDLE

ROUTE	GRADE	RATING	METERS	BOLTS	STYLE	Developed
7 Crusade Project	8a/+?		27m	10 bolts	Sport	2019

This route is destined to be a classic. Pristine rock, awesome movement... who is going to link it?

8 Kiss Kiss Bang Bang Project	8a/+?		25m	10 bolts	Sport	2019

Shares the last bolt and anchor with Khalas Project (9).

9 Khalas Project	8c?		25m	10 bolts	Sport	2019

Potentially the hardest route bolted thus far in the West Bank thanks to Michael Schreiber.

10 Serendipity Project	7c+?		24m	10 bolts	Sport	2019

Yet another project where brave climber can make history.

NABLUS | LEFT

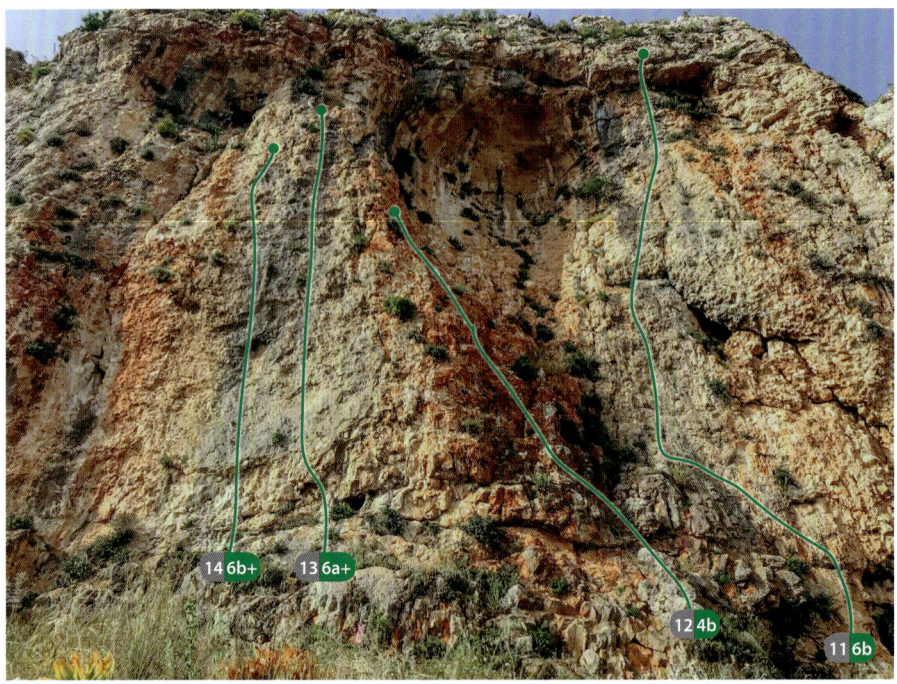

LEFT SIDE

ROUTE	GRADE	RATING	METERS	BOLTS	STYLE	DEVELOPED
11 Solace At Last	6b	★★★	28m	10 bolts	Sport	2018
Some routes take more than one try to get bolted (four to be precise). The longest route in Nablus!						
12 Hannes Konzept	4b		20m	8 bolts	Sport	2019
A good route for beginners and kids						
13 Nana (Mint)	6a+	★★	25m	8 bolts	Sport	2018
This route is part of the "herb trilogy." Also climb *Za'atar* (Thyme) in Yabrud and *Maramia* (Sage) in Ein Qiniya!						
14 Mr. Sinter	6b+	★★★	22m	7 bolts	Sport	2019
Tough spiky crimps and a Tufa. What more can you ask for?						

LEFT | NABLUS

LEFT

ROUTE	GRADE	RATING	METERS	BOLTS	STYLE	DEVELOPED
15 Balata Crack	6a	★★	20m	6 bolts	Sport	2019
Nice crack climbing — appreciate it, very rare in Palestine.						
16 Iron Gem	6a	★★	24m	10 bolts	Sport	2018
This route features lovely ironized holds.						
17 Drillerilla	5b		13m	5 bolts	Sport	2019
Nice warm-up route. 5a if you go up left after the third bolt.						
18 Sunset Prayer	5b		13m	4 bolts	Sport	2018
Enjoy the views on the city of Nablus while hearing the calls for prayer emanating from the city's old mosques resounding up the valley.						

Dario Franchetti lived in Palestine for many years and bolted tons of routes. Thank you for your contribution to Palestinian climbing, Dario!
Photo by Tim Bruns

INDEX BY ROUTE NAME

Route Name	Grade	Page Number	Location
140$	7a	106	Ein Fara
70 kph	6a	114	Ein Fara
A Friend from Down Unda'	4+	54	Ein Yabrud
A Plumber's Smile	6a+	77	New Ein Qiniya
A0 Approach	A0	108	Ein Fara
Adamantium	5a	42	Yabrud
Adi's Doctorate	6c+	112	Ein Fara
Adi's Doctorate Variation	6b	112	Ein Fara
Adventure Time	6c	44	Yabrud
Ahjee!	5c+	84	Al Bireh
Aibtisama	5c	142	Nablus
Al Hakim (Nathan der Weise)	7a	69	Ein Qiniya
Al Kasul	5c	85	Al Bireh
Al Qala'a (The Fortress)	6c+	54	Ein Yabrud
Al Quds	5a	122	Battir
Al Shatr Bidhak Fil Akhir	6a+	66	Ein Qiniya
Al-Osh	5b	66	Ein Qiniya
Alm Falastin	project	124	Battir
Alternative Facts	6c+	44	Yabrud
Ambicioso	6a	113	Ein Fara
Angry Birds	6a	65	Ein Qiniya
Areda	5b	119	Battir
Arik Is Thinking About It	6c+	108	Ein Fara
Arubota'im	6a	93	Ein Fara
Asal / Honey	5b	124	Battir
Athan	5c	75	New Ein Qiniya
Avada Kadabra	7a	43	Yabrud
Bab	6b	67	Ein Qiniya
Baba's Route	6a+	78	New Ein Qiniya
Balata Crack	6a	145	Nablus
Ballerina	6c	52	Ein Yabrud
Baloota	6a	30	Yabrud
Bater	5c	125	Battir
Batman	6c	99	Ein Fara
Beef Shoulder	6b+	104	Ein Fara
Beef Shoulder (pitch 2)	7c+	104	Ein Fara
Bergsteiger	5a	53	Ein Yabrud
Bes Sukar	6a	31	Yabrud
Better Nate Than Lever	6c	121	Battir
Bil Tawfiq (Good Luck)	6c	68	Ein Qiniya
Bim Bam Bam Tiras Ham	6b	114	Ein Fara

INDEX BY ROUTE NAME

Route Name	Grade	Page Number	Location
Blood Donor	5c	69	Ein Qiniya
Bloody Fingers	6b+	82	Al Bireh
Bomba	5b	105	Ein Fara
Border Run	6c+	104	Ein Fara
Border Run (pitch 2)	6b	104	Ein Fara
Border Run Variation	6b	104	Ein Fara
Butcher's Chunk	7a	104	Ein Fara
Butt vs. Gravity	6c+	66	Ein Qiniya
Cairo Slammer	7c	94	Ein Fara
Carlsbad	6a+	101	Ein Fara
Cave Line	6c+	129	Wadi Tamer
Cheesegrater (aka Kasereiber)	6c	68	Ein Qiniya
Children's Game	6b	93	Ein Fara
Chocolate Noir	6b	92	Ein Fara
Chris Shawarma Project	project	35	Yabrud
Circus Show	6a	44	Yabrud
Cocaine	7a+	93	Ein Fara
Convergence	6b	109	Ein Fara
Cops and Thieves	6a+	97	Ein Fara
Corner Crack	5a	113	Ein Fara
Cornflake	6c	65	Ein Qiniya
Crazy Dance	6b	68	Ein Qiniya
Crazy Orange	6a	99	Ein Fara
Criss Cross Hob	5b	30	Yabrud
Crossing Red Lines	8c	94	Ein Fara
Crusade Project	8a/+?	143	Nablus
Cry Me a Wadi	5c	76	New Ein Qiniya
Demolition Order	5c	78	New Ein Qiniya
Diagonal	6c+	109	Ein Fara
Diamond Mine	6c	42	Yabrud
Dio Santo	7a	95	Ein Fara
Diplomatic Status	6c	62	Ein Qiniya
Dirty Peter	7a+/7b	110	Ein Fara
Divergence	6b	109	Ein Fara
Don't Falafall	5c	142	Nablus
Dr. Evil and Mr. Hyde	7a	105	Ein Fara
Drillerilla	5b	145	Nablus
Dubke Dance	6a+	30	Yabrud
Dvivon (Racoon)	7c	108	Ein Fara
Face It!	7c	99	Ein Fara
Falastin	5a	119	Battir

INDEX BY ROUTE NAME

Route Name	Grade	Page Number	Location
Farasha / Butterfly	5c	125	Battir
Fayrouz Al Halwa	6b	65	Ein Qiniya
Feige Dattel	7c+	44	Yabrud
Fist Line	6a+	129	Wadi Tamer
Flash the Goat Hunter	6b+	114	Ein Fara
Fools Rush In	6a	76	New Ein Qiniya
Foxy Lady	6b+	52	Ein Yabrud
Gandalf's Eagle	6c	55	Ein Yabrud
Gandalf's Eagle Extension Project	P	55	Ein Yabrud
Gemini	6c+	100	Ein Fara
Goat Face Killa'	6c	38	Yabrud
Goats Are Cool	7a+	35	Yabrud
Goin' Back to Pali Project	project	35	Yabrud
Good New World	5c	92	Ein Fara
Hai Hilelik	5b	31	Yabrud
Hajiz	7a	120	Battir
Half an Avocado	6b+	40	Yabrud
Half Moon	5c+	84	Al Bireh
Hammurabi's Flute	6a	97	Ein Fara
Hamor Garem	6a+	114	Ein Fara
Hands of the Revolution	5b	92	Ein Fara
Hangman	6a	62	Ein Qiniya
Hanna Banana	5c	114	Ein Fara
Hannes Konzept	4b	144	Nablus
Hard for Today	6a+	35	Yabrud
Hei Hop	5c	114	Ein Fara
Henry's Project	project	35	Yabrud
Hidden Agenda	6b+	82	Al Bireh
High Expectations	7a+	79	New Ein Qiniya
Hofra One	5c	40	Yabrud
Hofra Two	6a	40	Yabrud
Holy Go Lightly	6c	40	Yabrud
Hot & Dumb	6c	115	Ein Fara
Hunch Back	5c	84	Al Bireh
Hyena	6a	119	Battir
Ice Tea	6b+	95	Ein Fara
Im Kztat Pilpel Bayashvan	6b+	115	Ein Fara
In Memory of Yoav Nir	8a+	96	Ein Fara
Iraqi Celebration	8a+	96	Ein Fara
Iron Gem	6a	145	Nablus
Islands in the Stream	7c+	109	Ein Fara

INDEX BY ROUTE NAME

Route Name	Grade	Page Number	Location
Israeli Tamer	V10	135	Wadi Tamer
Ivory Coast	4+	101	Ein Fara
Jamming in the Holy Land	6c	106	Ein Fara
Jeans Butt	5c	108	Ein Fara
Jehad J.	5b	123	Battir
Jeremiah	7c+	94	Ein Fara
Jeremiah Variation	7b+	95	Ein Fara
Jibril Rajub	7a+	101	Ein Fara
Jigsaw Puzzle	6b	97	Ein Fara
Jug-or-Not	5a	68	Ein Qiniya
July-August Heat	6c+	93	Ein Fara
Jumana's Smile	6a+	120	Battir
Just One Small Move More	6a+	92	Ein Fara
Kabus (Nightmare) Project	project	35	Yabrud
Kal Kar	6a	109	Ein Fara
Kalamantena	4a	122	Battir
Kalb / Heart	4b	124	Battir
Kareem Abdul Jabar	6a	64	Ein Qiniya
Khalas Project	8c?	143	Nablus
Khudra wa Fawakeh	6a	76	New Ein Qiniya
King of Vafunculo	7c+	108	Ein Fara
Kishkashta	7a	96	Ein Fara
Kiss Kiss Bang Bang Project	8a/+?	143	Nablus
Lady S	6a+	97	Ein Fara
Lady With Bags	6b+	99	Ein Fara
Land of Ooo	6b	44	Yabrud
Last Call	7b+	60	Ein Qiniya
Le Visionnaire	6a+	41	Yabrud
Life on the Edge	5c+	30	Yabrud
Lola	6a+	95	Ein Fara
Lola Variation	6b	95	Ein Fara
Long Espresso	7c	96	Ein Fara
Lucky Strike	6b+	100	Ein Fara
Lump	6b	75	New Ein Qiniya
Lunatics	5c+	77	New Ein Qiniya
Ma'arajaat	5c+	32	Yabrud
Madagascar	5b/5c	101	Ein Fara
Maikel's Balls	6c	65	Ein Qiniya
Maqlooba Dazed	6b	32	Yabrud
Maramia	5a	65	Ein Qiniya
Marcinalisation	5b+	76	New Ein Qiniya

INDEX BY ROUTE NAME

Route Name	Grade	Page Number	Location
Masar Ibrahim (Abraham's Path)	6c	55	Ein Yabrud
Mathew's Bush	6a+	52	Ein Yabrud
Mia fil Mia	7a+	32	Yabrud
Middleman	6b+	106	Ein Fara
Mixta Grill	7b+	108	Ein Fara
Mixta Grill Extension	7b+	108	Ein Fara
Modern Times	6a	112	Ein Fara
Moftah Alawda	6a	124	Battir
Momtaa	4c	122	Battir
More Atar Please	6b+	68	Ein Qiniya
Motaz	4b	119	Battir
Moza	4c+	122	Battir
Mr. Panino	7a	115	Ein Fara
Mr. Sinter	6b+	144	Nablus
Mutaarij	5b	83	Al Bireh
My Humps	6a+	35	Yabrud
Nablusi Soap	6a+	30	Yabrud
Naim Ve Tipusi	6a	99	Ein Fara
Nana (Mint)	6a+	144	Nablus
Nasheet Qamr	5c	119	Battir
Natif for the Poor	7a	110	Ein Fara
Neat and Petite	6a+/6b	53	Ein Yabrud
Nell and Oriol	6b	39	Yabrud
New Left	7b	94	Ein Fara
Nice and Uncomplicated	5b	142	Nablus
Nice Dude	V6	136	Wadi Tamer
No Contact Policy	project	70	Ein Qiniya
No Karsh Needed	6c	85	Al Bireh
No Name	5a	123	Battir
Northern Wind	6c	105	Ein Fara
Not Hard But Spiky	6c	115	Ein Fara
Now You See Me Now You Dont	5c	38	Yabrud
Nutcracked	5b	64	Ein Qiniya
Offwidth	6c+	129	Wadi Tamer
Oldie	6b	95	Ein Fara
On the Edge	5c	53	Ein Yabrud
One Flew Over the Cuckoo's Nest	7a+	44	Yabrud
One Move to Seventh Heaven	6c	38	Yabrud
One Move Wonder	7a	113	Ein Fara
Organ Donor	6a	69	Ein Qiniya
Organized Crime	7b	115	Ein Fara

INDEX BY ROUTE NAME

Route Name	Grade	Page Number	Location
Overhead Costs	6a+	82	Al Bireh
Pain in the Ass	7a+	106	Ein Fara
Palestinian White Boy	7c	43	Yabrud
Palifornia Dreamin'	6a+	35	Yabrud
Patience Palestine	5b	142	Nablus
Peril Roja	5c	114	Ein Fara
Pickpocket	7b	35	Yabrud
Pigs in Space	7a+	96	Ein Fara
Pillar	5b	113	Ein Fara
Pink Scarf	6b+	64	Ein Qiniya
PK 32	7b	99	Ein Fara
PK 34	7b	99	Ein Fara
Plastcine	5c+	92	Ein Fara
Pocket Pick	6b	84	Al Bireh
Pompa	6c	105	Ein Fara
Prickley Pair	5c	53	Ein Yabrud
Princess Bubblegum	4+	44	Yabrud
Prologue	6a	92	Ein Fara
Qalandia Crimper	6c+/7a	39	Yabrud
Raed	4c	119	Battir
Rambazamba	6c+	70	Ein Qiniya
Redemption at Last	6a+	142	Nablus
Rhino	6b	77	New Ein Qiniya
Ripped Pants	6a	38	Yabrud
Rotor	6b	109	Ein Fara
Russian Eagle	6b+	30	Yabrud
Russians in Space	8b+	96	Ein Fara
Sababsta	V4	133	Wadi Tamer
Sagur	5b	68	Ein Qiniya
Sahalia (Lizard)	6c	43	Yabrud
Sakher	4c	124	Battir
Salmonella	7a	97	Ein Fara
Saufen	6c	83	Al Bireh
Seba	5b+	119	Battir
Selim the Boar Hunter	6c+	54	Ein Yabrud
Serendipity Project	7c+?	143	Nablus
Shades of Beauty	6c	105	Ein Fara
Shades of Beauty Variation	7a	105	Ein Fara
Shai Ma Sukar	5c	31	Yabrud
Shajara	6a+	120	Battir
Sharq Face	6c	67	Ein Qiniya

INDEX BY ROUTE NAME

Route Name	Grade	Page Number	Location
Shawarma Blues	5c+	64	Ein Qiniya
Shmeltzy- Heee	project	100	Ein Fara
Shock	5c	101	Ein Fara
Short Espresso	6a+	95	Ein Fara
Slap that Hemar	6c	55	Ein Yabrud
Solace at Last	6b	144	Nablus
Solhafa's Shell	6b+	42	Yabrud
Solid Dude	V6	136	Wadi Tamer
Sometimes Difficult Never Impossible	7c+	106	Ein Fara
Soup of the Day	6c	101	Ein Fara
Spaced Out	6b	105	Ein Fara
Spare the Rod, Spoil the Route	6a	106	Ein Fara
Spread Eagle	5b	55	Ein Yabrud
State of Monk	6c+	99	Ein Fara
Steve	6a	77	New Ein Qiniya
Stroll	6a	100	Ein Fara
Stroll Direct	6c+	100	Ein Fara
Sukar Ma Shai	5c+	31	Yabrud
Sunset Prayer	5b	145	Nablus
Swingman	6b+	62	Ein Qiniya
Take Me to Deutschland	7a+	66	Ein Qiniya
Tannourine Dream	7b	35	Yabrud
Tasrih	6b	78	New Ein Qiniya
Tension	7a+	94	Ein Fara
Testa Rossa	5c	114	Ein Fara
The Accent	6a+	55	Ein Yabrud
The Accent Extension Project	project	55	Ein Yabrud
The Bullet and the Feather	7a	38	Yabrud
The Classic Waterfall Route	6a+	129	Wadi Tamer
The Corner	6c	113	Ein Fara
The Crying Game	7a	113	Ein Fara
The Dark Side of the Sun	6a+	32	Yabrud
The First Cut is the Deepest	6a	55	Ein Yabrud
The Flying Dutchman	6c+	62	Ein Qiniya
The Game of Thorns	5c+	53	Ein Yabrud
The Garden Crack	5c	95	Ein Fara
The Goat's Hairdresser	5c+	52	Ein Yabrud
The Last Mohican	project	100	Ein Fara
The Monk	6a	99	Ein Fara
The New Chapter	6a+	77	New Ein Qiniya

INDEX BY ROUTE NAME

Route Name	Grade	Page Number	Location
The Next Century	6b+	30	Yabrud
The Nile	5b/5c	101	Ein Fara
The Nun	6a	99	Ein Fara
The Pearl	6b	79	New Ein Qiniya
The Peg	6b+	94	Ein Fara
The Perfect Boulder	project	101	Ein Fara
The Pillar (left)	6a	130	Wadi Tamer
The Pillar (pitch 2a)	5c	130	Wadi Tamer
The Pillar (pitch 2b)	5c	130	Wadi Tamer
The Pillar (right)	6b+	130	Wadi Tamer
The Prophecy	7a+	110	Ein Fara
The Suitcase	7b	97	Ein Fara
The Thief's Road	7a	42	Yabrud
The Tomb	6c	110	Ein Fara
The Virgin	6a	99	Ein Fara
The Whore	6a+	99	Ein Fara
This Week in Palestine	6c+	54	Ein Yabrud
Thoma wa Bassal	5c+	41	Yabrud
Three Month Fling	6b+	54	Ein Yabrud
Tofah	4b	122	Battir
Too Hard For Today	7a+	82	Al Bireh
Traditional Modern Times	5b	112	Ein Fara
Trou du Cul	7b+	60	Ein Qiniya
Um	5b	75	New Ein Qiniya
Unknown	6c?	115	Ein Fara
Unknown	8a?	115	Ein Fara
Unknown	6a	115	Ein Fara
Unknown	7c?	115	Ein Fara
Unknown	7c?	115	Ein Fara
Unknown	7c?	115	Ein Fara
Unnamed	project	119	Battir
Unnamed	7a+	99	Ein Fara
Unnamed	7a+	99	Ein Fara
Unnamed	6a	99	Ein Fara
Unnamed	5b/ 5c	100	Ein Fara
Unnamed	7a	102	Ein Fara
Unnamed	6b+	102	Ein Fara
Unnamed	6a	102	Ein Fara
Unnamed	6a	106	Ein Fara
Unnamed	7a	115	Ein Fara
Unnamed	7c	115	Ein Fara

INDEX BY ROUTE NAME

Route Name	Grade	Page Number	Location
Unnamed	7a+	129	Wadi Tamer
Unnamed	5b	129	Wadi Tamer
Unnamed	6a+	130	Wadi Tamer
Unnamed	V6	133	Wadi Tamer
Unnamed	V5	135	Wadi Tamer
Unnamed	V2	135	Wadi Tamer
Unnamed	V2	135	Wadi Tamer
Unnamed	V3	136	Wadi Tamer
Unnamed	V4	136	Wadi Tamer
Unnamed	V5	136	Wadi Tamer
Unnamed	V5	133	Wadi Tamer
Unnamed	V5	134	Wadi Tamer
Unnamed	V4	134	Wadi Tamer
Unnamed	V3	134	Wadi Tamer
Unnamed	V3	134	Wadi Tamer
Unnamed Project	project	52	Ein Yabrud
Unnamed Variation	7b	99	Ein Fara
Up and Over	6c	55	Ein Yabrud
Valhalla	7b	62	Ein Qiniya
Ventilator	6b	113	Ein Fara
Viper Palestinae	6b	38	Yabrud
Wade	5a	124	Battir
Walk the Line	5b	41	Yabrud
Walking In Sunshine	4c	123	Battir
Warda	6a	125	Battir
Waterfall (easy start)	6a	129	Wadi Tamer
Waterfall (hard start)	7b	129	Wadi Tamer
West Bank Only	6b+	78	New Ein Qiniya
Where Is The Drill Bit?	6a	30	Yabrud
Wild Boar	6a+	83	Al Bireh
Will Climb for Donor Money	6b	65	Ein Qiniya
Yakir Mi Paz	6b	99	Ein Fara
Yalla Yalla	6a	142	Nablus
Yom Asel	6a+	62	Ein Qiniya
Yonatan Shapiro	7b+	106	Ein Fara
Za'atar	5b	39	Yabrud
Zawia (The Corner)	6a	67	Ein Qiniya
Zift Maqli (Boiled Asphalt)	6b+	78	New Ein Qiniya
Zinab's Curse	6c+	79	New Ein Qiniya

NOTES

MAP LEGEND

Natural Features
- 🟥 Climbing Area
- ⋯ Contour Line
- ━ Wet Wadi
- - - - Dry Wadi

Political Boundaries
- Oslo Area A/B
- Oslo Area C
- ━━━━ '49 Armistice Line
- Palestinian Locality
- Israeli Settlement/Outpost
- Israeli Military Area
- Israeli Nature Reserve

Infrastructure
- ━━ Highway
- ━━ Major Road
- ━ Local Road
- ----- Unpaved Road
- ----- Established Hiking Path
- .... Climber's Track
- ⊥⊥⊥⊥⊥ Separation Wall
- ⊗ Major Checkpoint
- ⊗ Diplomatic Access Checkpoint
- ⊗ Other Limited Access Checkpoint
- ⊖ Nature Reserve Entry Point
- ⊖ Israeli Settlement Entry Point
- ✕ Road Block
- ✕ Temporary Block or Checkpoint
- ∥ Tunnel/Underpass
- 🅿 Parking Area
- ⊕ Hospital/Medical Centre
- ⋮⋮ Building Ruins
- ★ Other Landmark

Map Disclaimer: The information used to create the maps in this guidebook stems from a variety of sources with varying accuracy, resolutions, and temporal validity. Also, Palestine is a dynamic space with major construction and continuously-changing access due to the occupation (e.g. through road closures, flying checkpoints, barriers, and Separation Wall construction by the Israeli military). In order to make the maps more user-friendly, the information has been simplified. Some of the roads displayed on the maps may be limited to private or military use, or accessible with 4WD only (particularly in the case of unpaved roads). We recommend seeking updated access information (e.g. through UN OCHA or from local climbers) prior to visiting some of the climbing sites, and to use these maps in conjunction with online maps services such as Open Street Maps or Google Maps. We've done our best to make the maps as accurate as possible under difficult geopolitical circumstances.

Photo by Marion Ponserre

Two climbers sharing a moment in Yabrud
Photo by Henna Taylor